LIBRARY

This book is to be returned on or above the last date stamped below. Fines will be charged for books returned late.

UNIVERSITY COLLEGE CHESTER
A College of the University of Liverpool

A & C Black · London

First published 1991 by
A & C Black (Publishers) Ltd
35 Bedford Row, London WC1R 4JH

Reprinted 1995

© 1991 Geoff Cooke

ISBN 0 7136 3444 8

A CIP catalogue record for this book
is available from the British Library.

Distributed in the USA by
The Talman Company
131 Spring Street
New York, NY 10012.

Typeset by Latimer Trend & Company Ltd, Plymouth

Printed and bound in Great Britain by
Whitstable Litho Printers Ltd, Whitstable, Kent

CONTENTS

INTRODUCTION

There have been many instructional books about Rugby Union, but most of them have been aimed at the coach or teacher. This book is written primarily for the benefit of players, particularly those playing at club and school 1st-xv level, though there is much in the content that should be of value to coaches and teachers.

You cannot learn to play any game well just by reading a book, but having been introduced to rugby and gained some experience, you can improve your play through greater understanding of the game. Deeper knowledge and appreciation of the key factors of individual and unit skills as well as the underlying principles of play will help you to practise constructively and play more effectively.

The aim of this book is to increase your awareness and appreciation and, although many points of technique are described, the emphasis throughout is on why and when to do something rather than how to do it. Strategy, tactics and team play are dealt with only briefly

and in general terms, and there are no details of practices that can be used to develop the various skills. Such elements are specific to the particular needs of you and your team, and it is the job of your club or school coach to guide you in these matters.

Be sure, however, to regard your coach only as an adviser. He must not be a dictator, and you must not be a puppet with someone else pulling the strings. Rugby is a thinking person's game. Do not expect someone else to tell you exactly what to do and when to do it during a match. In rugby, players constantly have to make decisions for themselves. The best players are those who make the right decisions most often.

I hope this book will cause you to think about your play, perhaps in a way you have never done before; that it will help you and your team to improve the quality of your rugby and, by doing so, add to your enjoyment of a wonderful game.

TEAM PLAY

Objectives

Rugby Union is a team game, and your objectives should be to win every match and ensure that all 15 players are involved in an enjoyable and satisfying manner. Each player must feel that he has a responsible part to play, and the individual character and ability of each player must not be suffocated by the attacking and defensive organisation of your team. Team organisation must simply provide a framework within which the players can perform their individual, positional and unit skills in trying to score more points than their opponents.

Score points

The overall aim of the game is to score more points than the opposition. You can score tries, drop goals and penalty goals. However, you cannot control the award of penalties in kickable positions, so tries and drop goals must be your preferred options.

To score tries and drop goals you must have possession of the ball, and to give you the best chance of scoring, you must have the right sort of possession at the right time and in the right position.

That possession must then be used effectively, with players making the right decisions and carrying out the necessary skills at pace.

Possession

The set pieces – scrums, line-outs, re-starts – are the primary source of possession. You must be able to win ball securely from set pieces. Although the forwards are the main ball winners, all players have a responsibility to secure, retain or regain possession. Having secured possession, it then must be retained (ideally) until your team has scored. Remember, when you kick the ball you immediately give away hard-earned possession.

The ball must also be kept under your control; it should never go back towards your line apart from in a controlled, purposeful manner. You must also recognise how the source and quality of possession enhances or limits your options.

Position

You must identify the positions on the field that give your team the best chance of scoring tries or drop goals: for example, a dynamic ruck/maul in your opponents' 22m area with their defence disorganised, or any scrum within 22m of their line on your put-in.

If these are your agreed objectives you should then organise your team play to reach these positions and control possession of the ball.

Depending on the starting point, you may have to go through three or four phases of play to establish these positions but, as long as everyone in the team understands the objectives and you have the skill to keep the ball, it doesn't matter how long it takes.

Purpose

Everyone must therefore know and understand the team's objectives from all phases of play in all areas of the field. Everyone must also have a positive attitude, i.e. you must set out to make things happen rather than simply react to what your opponents are doing.

Pace

A former New Zealand coach, Freddie Allen,

once remarked that 'there is an answer to everything in rugby, except pace'! How right he was. If you can run faster, think faster and move the ball faster than your opponents, you will have a distinct advantage.

But pace must be controlled and your team should try to dictate the pace of the game; this generally should be as fast as possible, without losing that vital control of the ball, of your thoughts, of your body positions, or of your discipline.

Principles

In achieving these objectives, there are six important principles to observe.

Go forwards

Every player knows that to score points you have to get the ball over your opponents' goal-line, and every player knows in which direction he is supposed to be playing. It is amazing, therefore, how much time players spend running across the field towards the touch-lines or, worse still, back towards their own goal-line. This sort of running makes winning rugby difficult to achieve, even though the laws demand that on occasions the ball must go back before you can begin to move it forwards. Go forwards it must, however, and the important thing is to select your method of progress according to the situation.

The only way to move the ball forwards towards your opponents' goal-line is to carry it or kick it. If you kick it you immediately lose possession and give your opponents a chance to move the ball towards your line. Running and carrying the ball must therefore be your first choice of method of progress so that your opponents have to stop you to prevent a score.

Ball-carrier in front

The second and perhaps most important principle of play is to work to get a ball-carrier in front of the rest of your team and ideally behind at least the first line of your opponents' defence. This can be achieved in many ways, e.g. by your No. 8 picking up from the base of a scrum and quickly attacking down the right-hand side of the pitch; by a line-out peel and drive; by a mid-field player beating his immediate opponent; by a high kick and chase,

Ball carrier in front

Support either side

catching the receiver in possession and recovering the ball from him; or by tackling an opponent behind his own forwards and stripping the ball from him. Whichever tactics you employ, the longer you can keep a ball-carrier in front of the rest of your team, the more scoring chances you will create.

Support

Having achieved the second objective, you must then work to get support to the ball-carrier coming from depth at pace. Support covers a multitude of situations in attack and defence, but the focal point of support is always the ball-carrier. The principal elements of effective support are speed (timing), position and amount.

You should always try to achieve support on each side of the ball-carrier, and within five metres of him at least one support player should be running parallel to the touch-lines. Always try to get more players within five metres of the

ball than your opponents have. Positive running without the ball is just as important as running with the ball.

Continuity

Now it is important to maintain the continuity of play, ideally until you score. Your opponents will not just let this happen, of course, and ball-carriers will be tackled. If one route is blocked, another must be found, and this is where passing comes into play; you must move the ball to a player who can continue to carry it forwards into space. If you fail to maintain this continuity, your opponents may wrestle the ball from you or the referee may whistle for a scrum or line-out, and the opposition will have a chance to regain possession.

You must try to deny them these opportunities by keeping the ball moving and in play. Rucks and mauls should be regarded as temporary interruptions to your forward progress, and your team must be proficient at keeping the ball 'alive' in these situations.

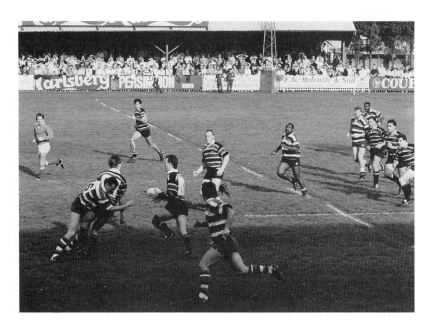

When checked, try to keep the ball moving

Control

Control is an essential ingredient in all aspects of play. In many situations 'discipline' might be a more appropriate word. Self-control, control of the ball and control of other players in unit situations are typical examples of control in the game.

Control applies to handling, running, kicking, contact skills and positional play. No matter how well-organised and skilful your team is, without control there will be chaos.

Every match has certain critical phases when the need for control is paramount. These are normally the first and last ten minutes, ten minutes before and after half-time, and immediately following a score by either team.

Pressure

If you get the ball moving forwards through a ball-carrier who is in front of the rest of your team, and you can provide support from depth at pace and maintain continuity under control, you will certainly put your opponents under extreme pressure. By carrying the ball at them, forcing them to tackle, and by not kicking to touch unless absolutely necessary, they will be committed to desperate defence.

A team under pressure is more likely to make mistakes than a team with plenty of time to think and act, but you must sustain pressure if it is to be really effective. In attack, it must be sustained until your team scores, and in defence it must be maintained until you have regained possession without conceding a score.

If you do not have the ball, make it as difficult as possible for your opponents to win good possession. Even if they succeed, make it extremely difficult for them to use the ball effectively. Sustain pressure by denying them space and time, through sound defensive organisation and ruthlessly efficient tackling, and by not conceding penalties. Make them work hard for every scrap of possession and every gain of territory.

How do you want to play?

Observing principles will not necessarily produce satisfaction and enjoyment from a game of rugby. Your attitude to the game is the real key to success.

The very essence of rugby is running with and handling the ball. A player with the ball trying to run past a defender, sometimes succeeding, often being tackled, is the basic art of the sport. For anyone who watches, the most vivid

Pressure—the defence is poised

memories are likely to be those of tries being scored from flowing handling movements, or recollection of a particular player beating opponent after opponent in an exciting dash for the line.

If they are honest, most players, even the forwards, will probably admit that this is the type of rugby they also want to play. Every prop outwardly cherishes his own private battle in scrum, line-out, ruck and maul, but secretely he nurses a burning ambition to do a side-step, sell a dummy, or be involved in a handling movement that leads to a try being scored. This should also be what you want, so base your team play on this philosophy, with three simple aims:

1. to win possession of the ball
2. to keep possession of the ball
3. to score more tries than your opponents.

Decision making

The six principles of play provide a basis on which your team can operate, but how do you apply these principles in trying to achieve your objectives?

The first essential is to adopt a flexible approach to each match based on awareness and appreciation of what happens on the field, followed by an appropriate reaction to each particular situation as it arises. Don't try to play rugby as if it were a game of chess, by assuming that certain pre-planned moves in attack and defence will be met by predictable responses from your opponents.

Every player has to have the ability and willingness to make decisions as and when necessary. The best players are those who make the right decisions quickest and most often. It follows from this that all players must have a range of skills and techniques at their command from which to make their choice according to the situation. At first this range will be fairly limited, but as skill and experience increase so will the range develop. There is very little in rugby that is necessarily right or wrong in terms of technique. The criterion for any action is 'does it work?'. When and why you do something is generally far more important than how you do it.

Basic individual techniques

Rugby Union football is a combination of four basic elements: handling, running, kicking and body contact. Within each element a player needs a variety of techniques and skills.

Technique is the method by which an action is performed, and the effective use of an appropriate technique in the game is regarded as skill. The range of techniques and the level of mastery needed vary according to the different positional requirements, but all players should strive to be competent in the four basic elements. No single technique is appropriate for every circumstance and you must have a range of options at your command from which to select according to the demands of the situation. At first your range should be limited; don't try to achieve too much too soon. It is better to be very competent at one or two things than barely adequate in a great many. As your skill and experience increase, you should try to extend your capabilities.

Handling

All players require the general ability to handle the ball efficiently in various situations. The skills of handling can be broadly classified as passing, catching, picking up and carrying.

Passing

Passing is merely the transfer of the ball from one player to another, and though there are many ways of giving a pass, the most important yardstick is: does the ball arrive safely at its destination?

There must also be a good reason for every pass given. That reason could be:

1. to transfer the ball to a player in a better position
2. to create space for a team-mate
3. to deceive an opponent
4. to prevent the opposition from gaining possession.

Passing the ball

There is, therefore, the additional criterion of effectiveness: does the pass achieve its objectives? The actual method of passing is merely a means to an end. Different objectives require appropriate techniques. 'Why?' must be your first thought when you are about to pass the ball, closely followed by 'when?'; and you must also consider how your pass will be affected by the speed you impart to the ball, the height and angle of release, the length of pass and the air resistance encountered on the way. Only then can you really choose which pass to make and, as this decision will have to be made in a split second during a game, you must obviously practise all types of pass in a variety of circumstances.

Despite the many variables, there are certain key principles to observe.

1. How: Hold the ball in two hands, half-way down its sides.
   Why: It is the easiest way to hold the ball and it is usually the way you will catch or pick up the ball, therefore it avoids the need for re-adjustment.
2. How: Your fingers should be spread and relaxed.
   Why: It is essential for good control.
3. How: Look at the person you are passing to.
   Why: You need information. How far away is

he? Is he still or moving? Is there anybody in the way?
4. How: Your pass should arrive at chest height, to the front of the receiver.
   Why: It is the easiest position for catching. He can see the ball without lowering his eyes and can also see what is happening in front and to the side.

'Swing your arms' is a much-used coaching point for passing, but in reality the amount of arm swing depends upon the nature of the pass. Often a wrist flick or a pushing movement is more appropriate than a swing, and therefore arm movement is not included in the list of principles.

When giving a pass, the hand further from the target is your control hand. Giving a pass to the left is therefore easier for most players (being right-handed) than passing to the right. It is important to emphasise practice with your weaker hand, particularly when the ability to give long passes is required. Long passes need more arm movement than short passes, with your control hand in contact with the ball for as long as possible.

Although the laws of rugby oblige you to pass the ball backwards, an object of the game is to go forwards. Passes should normally be made as near to parallel with the goal-lines as

Pass at chest height

the laws permit. The general rule is 'pass sideways – run forwards', but remember, there are times when it is better to pass backwards, e.g. to give the receiver more time and space away from opponents.

Remember also that in wind your passes must generally be firmer and must allow for the effects of wind direction. Passes with the wind behind should be slightly higher, and ones against the wind should start slightly lower than usual. In wet conditions all passes should be rather softer and more lobbed than usual.

There are a number of well-known, named passes and these are described in the subsequent paragraphs. They are not the only ways of passing, however, and none of them may be appropriate in a particular circumstance. Very often an improvised pass is necessary, and you should practise transferring the ball in many different ways from a variety of situations.

Basic lateral pass

When and why: You have plenty of time. The receiver is running roughly parallel to you at the moment of decision.

How: If the receiver is running straight or drifting away from you, give a fast, flat pass. If he is close to you or coming in towards you, give a slower, lobbed pass.

One-pace pass

When and why: You have not yet received the ball but will need to move it on very quickly because of pressure from opponents or to exploit space outside you. Passing distance will be relatively short. The receiver must be running parallel to you.

How: Reach and take the ball early outside your shoulder width. Move your arms across your body quickly but release the ball relatively slowly.

An improvised pass may be necessary

Below Long passes may be needed

Basic lateral pass

One-pace pass sequence

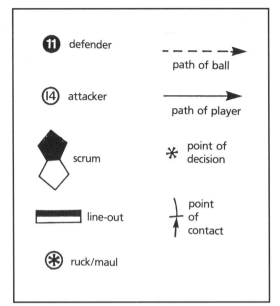

Key to diagrams

11 defender	- - - → path of ball
14 attacker	→ path of player
⬠ scrum	✱ point of decision
▬ line-out	⊥ point of contact
✳ ruck/maul	

Switch pass

When and why: To wrong-foot defenders, or to change the direction or point of attack. The receiver is initially on a parallel line of running, e.g. the right centre, moving towards the right touch-line, brings the right-wing infield with a switch pass.

How: Look at the receiver at all times. Change your line of running and accelerate across in front of him. Turn the ball towards him and give a short, soft pass from extended arms.

N.B. If you maintain your running line the receiver must move across and behind you.

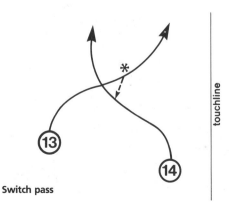

Switch pass

Loop pass

When and why: To create an extra-player situation, i.e. to put the loop runner into a gap between defenders. For example, the fly-half passes to the inside centre, than runs round behind him to receive the return pass. The centre is initially standing 'flat' on the fly-half.

How: The fly-half moves towards the centre and gives a slow and slightly lobbed pass. The centre must hold a straight line of running and give a one-pace pass as the fly-half loops round behind him.

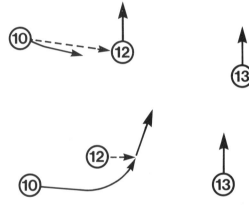

Loop pass

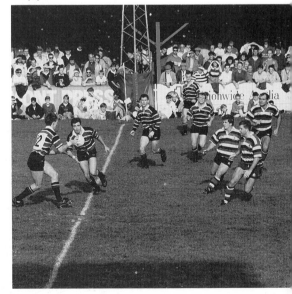

The start of a loop pass

Screen pass or pop pass

When and why: When you are driving forwards into contact with an opponent, to switch the defence target and maintain the continuity of the attack in close-contact situations. The receiver must be very close on a parallel running line.

How: Unbalance your immediate opponent by a slight feint or actual change of direction. If contact is unavoidable, drive in low, aiming at his outside hip. Ensure good control of the ball as contact is made. Give a short, lobbed pass just on contact or slightly before.

Dummy pass

When and why: To deceive an opponent. When the defender is anticipating a pass and is already moving towards the receiver.

How: The dummy could be applied to any of the above passes. The ball is held at the point of release and brought back into close control. In all other aspects it must look like an actual pass.

Passing faults

Fault
1. Passes are consistently too high.
2. Passes are consistently too low.
3. You are unable to make a long pass to your right.
4. Passes often go forwards.
5. Passes go behind or to the side of the receiver.
6. You are unable to make a one-pace pass.
7. Passes with wind drop short of the target.
8. Passes into wind drop short of the target.
9. Passes into wind balloon over the target.
10. Switch pass falls between the passer and receiver.
11. You are unable to 'sell a dummy'.

Probable cause
1. You are letting go of the ball too late.
2. You are letting go of the ball too early.
3. You have a weak left hand and/or poor hand position on the ball.
4. You are not turning your shoulders towards the target.
5. You are passing too deep or the receiver is too flat.

Selling a 'dummy'

6. Poor catching technique – you are not taking the ball early outside the width of your shoulders.
7. You are not adding extra lift to compensate for wind effect.
8. You are releasing the ball too high on a flat trajectory.
9. The pass is too soft and is released too high on an upward trajectory.
10. You are not turning the ball towards the receiver and watching it into his hands.
11. The opponent is not anticipating a pass: the dummy is therefore the wrong decision. You are not looking at the receiver. You are not fully completing the passing action up to the point of release.

Catching

Catching is simply the action of receiving the ball travelling through the air towards you by gradually slowing its momentum until it is held under control. No single method of catching is applicable to all situations, and you must have a range of techniques at your command.

Before selecting a method of catching you must consider the speed and direction of the ball, the height at which it will arrive, any spin affecting the flight, and the effects of elements such as wind, rain or mud. You must also be thinking about what happens next after catching the ball. If you have to pass it on quickly or kick under pressure this should determine the way you catch it. As these decisions have to be made very quickly in a game, it is essential to practise catching in different ways and in varying situations. Such practice can normally be combined with passing and kicking practices.

Whatever technique is being used, there are certain key principles to observe.

1. How: Watch the player kicking or passing the ball to you.
   Why: His body position will give you prior information about the type of kick or pass and the timing (when it is coming).
2. How: Watch the ball.
   Why: You need more information. How fast and how high is the pass? Is there any spin on the ball? Is the ball wet or dry?

3. How: Get behind the ball with your body or one or two hands.
   Why: The objective is to stop the flight of the ball.
4. How: Reach towards the ball with the largest possible area possible, i.e. fingers spread.
   Why: You must reduce the speed of the ball gradually to avoid rebounds. You must 'give' with the ball, and a large area helps to dissipate the force.
5. How: Turn your shoulders and chest towards the kicker or passer.
   Why: It makes hand and arm movements easier.

The different catching techniques are outlined below.

Lateral pass, spin pass or dive pass

When and why: You have plenty of time. The ball is travelling across the catcher's line of running.
   How: Elbows must be bent to provide 'give'. Your inside hand (further from the ball) should be in line with the flight. The fingers of both hands are spread and slightly flexed. Take the pace off the ball by:

1. taking it early with the hands and bringing it into the body
2. taking it across the chest and then moving away along the path of the ball.

One-pace pass or loop pass

When and why: You need to move the ball on very quickly.
   How: The hands and arms are as above. Take the ball early outside your shoulder width. In one movement, bring the ball across your body and send it on its way. Try to maintain the speed of the ball.

Switch pass

When and why: The passer is moving across and in front of the receiver, or the receiver is moving across and behind the passer.

How: Reach both hands under and beyond the ball, with your fingers well spread. Pull the ball into your chest and adjust, if necessary, for the next phase of action.

Screen pass or pop pass

When and why: Driving forwards into contact to receive a very short lob pass.

How: Bend well forwards from your waist and take the ball either:

1. as for the switch pass
2. by reaching your near arm over and beyond your outside arm, under and beyond the ball, to pull it into your body.

High, dropping kick

When and why: When you have plenty of time.

How: Take a firm stance with your feet slightly wider than your shoulders, and with your knees slightly flexed. Reach towards the ball with your fingers spread and your hands below and slightly across the path of the ball. Turn your thumbs out and tuck your elbows in. Take pace off the ball by bringing it down to your body. Dropping your knees slightly and turning your body will help this further if necessary.

When and why: When you are about to be tackled.

How: As above, but turn your hip towards the oncoming tackler and, as you take the ball, turn your upper body towards your own line.

When and why: When you need to make a kick quickly under pressure.

How: As above, but make sure that you turn towards the nearest touch-line.

Catching faults

Fault

1. Passes are dropped sideways or backwards.
2. Passes are going straight across your body.
3. Persistent knock-ons.
4. You are unable to pass the ball on quickly.
5. The ball rebounds from your chest.
6. High kicks are dropped.

Probable cause

1. Poor positioning – not enough depth to allow the passer to put the ball in front of you. You are not turning your shoulders towards the ball. You are snatching at the ball.
2. You are not getting your control hand behind the ball.
3. There is too much tension in your fingers – they are not spread and relaxed. There is no flexion at the elbows. You are not watching the ball. You are snatching at the ball. Your fingers are pointing at the ball.
4. You are taking it early outside your shoulder width.
5. You are not reaching out with your hands behind the ball.
6. Poor positioning – you are not under the ball with your elbows tucked in, and your fingers spread. You are not reaching up to take the ball early and take the pace off it gradually.

In every instance the fault could be not watching the kicker/passer or the ball.

Picking up

There are many occasions during a game when you will have to secure a ball on the ground. The skill of picking up requires a number of techniques to cover a variety of circumstances. The choice of method will depend primarily on the amount of time available and whether the ball is moving or stationary. You must also think about what you are going to do once you have got the ball and must take into account weather and ground conditions.

The key principles are as follows.

1. How: Watch the ball.
   Why: You need information. What is your distance from the ball? Is it lying end-on or side-on to you? Is it rolling or bouncing towards, away from or across you? Is it wet or dry?
2. How: Secure the ball with the largest possible area, i.e. two hands with fingers spread.
   Why: It is the most efficient method (try shovelling sand with a stick!).

The different techniques for picking up a ball are outlined below.

Stationary ball (going forwards)

When and why: You have plenty of time but the defenders are ahead.

How: Put one foot beyond the ball and half-turn towards your own goal-line. Bend your knees into a squat to give yourself a strong, balanced position and place your hands on either side of the ball, with fingers well spread. Lift the ball straight up to your body and look to pass to the first support player.

When and why: You have plenty of time, and there is no one beyond the ball.

How: Approach from the side in a low crouch position. Place the control hand, with fingers spread, on the near side of the ball, and your other hand on the far side. Scoop the ball with momentum into two hands and continue running.

When and why: Under pressure from opponents.

How: Either use method 1, or fall beyond the ball to put your body between the ball and the defenders. Secure the ball with two hands, and look to pass to the first support player or get up immediately.

Stationary ball (going back or sideways)

When and why: You have plenty of time.

How: Use the second method for a stationary ball (going forwards).

When and why: You are under pressure from an opponent.

How: Fall to put your body between the ball and the opposition. Secure the ball with two hands and get up immediately.

Ball rolling towards you

When and why: You have plenty of time.

How: Stop the ball with your feet, then pick it up as in the first method for a stationary ball (going forwards).

When and why: When under pressure from opponents.

How: Fall as in the third method for a stationary ball (going forwards), stopping the ball with your hands and arms as it passes under your falling body. Get up immediately.

Ball rolling away from you

When and why: You have plenty of time.

How: Fall as in the third method for a stationary ball (going forwards).

When and why: Under pressure from opponents.

How: Fall as above.

When and why: In wet conditions.

How: Fall as above.

Picking-up faults

Fault

1. You are fumbling the pick-up.
2. You are over-running the ball.
3. You are losing control when falling on the ball.

Probable cause

1. You are not watching the ball. You have a poor body position. You are not putting your hands on opposite sides of the ball. You are snatching at the ball.
2. You are not watching the ball. You have a poor body position – especially not bending the knees. Your hands are too high on the ball.
3. You have poor body position. You are not securing the ball in two hands before your body hits the ground.

N.B. Most pick-up faults are due to wrong choice of technique.

Carrying

There are basically four ways in which the ball can be carried:

Carry the ball under control

1. in two hands, away from your body
2. in two hands, close to your body
3. with one hand and arm, close to your body
4. in one hand only, away from your body.

The fourth method is suitable only for players with large hands, and in dry conditions. No single method is suitable for every situation, and you should develop your ability in the first three methods.

Keeping the ball under control is the most important aspect of carrying and, in selecting the technique to use in any situation, your main concerns should be what is likely to happen next and what options are available to you. Nearly all carrying faults appear as loss of control, usually in contact situations though sometimes in the process of adjusting the ball from one hand and arm to two hands. In every case, the fault is probably caused by wrong initial choice of technique in the circumstances.

Two hands

When and why: Running with the ball but likely to have to give a pass at any moment.

How: Place your hands on either side of the ball, with fingers spread and relaxed. Point your elbows out and press your hands in. Hold the ball away from you at chest height.

When and why: Driving forwards with the ball in close-contact situations, ready to screen pass or make the ball available to support players.

How: Hands and fingers are as above but with firm control. The elbows are more tucked in but the hands are still pressing inwards. The ball is held close to your body at about hip height. Lean forwards from the waist, with one shoulder leading.

One hand and arm

When and why: Running in space, no pressure from any opponent.

How: One hand is on the side of the ball, with fingers spread and hand and forearm pressing the ball to the chest. The free arm assists the running speed.

When and why: Running in space but with pressure from one opponent.

How: As above, but the free arm is ready to hand-off a defender or add to control of the ball if necessary.

When and why: Driving forwards in close-contact situations.

How: Hand and arm contact is as in the first method but the ball is at waist height. The free arm is used to fend off opponents.

One hand only

When and why: This method is only for players with large hands, and in dry conditions. When running in space with pressure from one opponent, it keeps the ball out of the tackle area.

How: The fingers of one hand are spread and grip the side of the ball towards one end.

Running

Although running ability is so obviously important in rugby, it is surprising how few players pay attention to this aspect of their game. Most of the running you do in practice is either as part of fitness training or incidental to the development of other skills. Yet all players, regardless of position, have to be able to run at different speeds and change direction as and when required. The only real difference between levels of ability in these skills is speed, and the relative need for pace depends upon your playing position and the standard of rugby you play.

The speed at which you can run is determined by the length of your stride and the number of strides you take in a given time. Your rate of striding can be improved by training, but your stride length is largely governed by your physique. Nevertheless, you can probably improve your stride if you concentrate on really

extending your rear leg through the hip, knee and ankle joints to obtain maximum forward drive.

However, because the running techniques that give greatest speed are different from those that enable changes of direction to be made readily, your running must be something of a compromise. Your ability to change speed and direction depends on the force you can exert on the ground through your feet and the speed with which you can do this. Control must therefore be your keyword, and you will rarely run absolutely flat out during a game. What happens next should be your main criterion in determining how to run in any specific situation.

Remember, however, that running in all its forms is a natural ability and you must not become too conscious of technique.

Changing speed

Accelerating

When and why: From a standing start, e.g. the centre going up to tackle from the scrum.

How: Short, fast strides, gradually increasing in length until the desired speed is reached. Use the ball of the foot only. Don't try to exaggerate your stride length as speed increases, as this often leads to muscle injuries (hamstring strain).

When and why: From coasting speed, e.g. the wing takes a pass from the centre and goes to beat his opponent on the outside or checks as a

Elusive running needs change of pace and direction

tackler comes in, then accelerates as the tackler hesitates.

How: Shorten your stride length slightly and increase the rate of striding. As speed increases, your stride will lengthen and the rate of striding will level off.

Decelerating

When and why: Slowing for control in preparation for the next piece of action, e.g. making a kick.

How: Ease off effort. Swing your lower leg forwards for braking effect, using the full sole and heel of the foot.

Changing direction

Basic

When and why: To alter the line of running at relatively low speeds.

How: Press hard on the foot through the leg more nearly opposite your desired direction of movement.

Side-step

When and why: To change direction very sharply to deceive an opponent.

How: For a side-step to your left, control your pace and shorten your stride length. Drop your

body weight on to your bent right leg and drive away to the left with a wide step off your left leg. Your upper body must feint to go right and you must not get too close to your opponent.

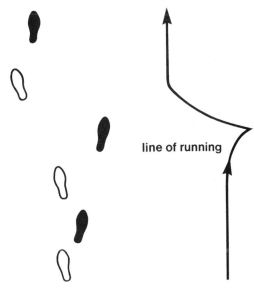

line of running

Side step

Swerve

When and why: To change direction smoothly at relatively high speeds.

How: For a swerve to your left, feint to the right with a slight turn of your shoulders as your left foot goes forwards. Then make a long stride

Changing direction

across your running line with your right leg and allow your body to fall away to the left as your left leg follows through.

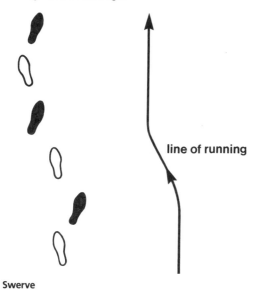

line of running

Swerve

Kicking

Despite the fact that rugby is basically a handling game, kicking is an important part of it. The level of kicking ability needed by players varies according to positional requirements, but every player should have some basic skill.

There are two main types of kick:

1. from your hands
2. from the ground.

Although there a number of ways of making these kicks, the ultimate result of any kick depends upon the speed, height and angle at which the ball leaves the kicker's foot, and on the resistance encountered in flight.

Your choice of a specific technique will depend upon the objective of your kick, except when the method is determined by the laws of the game, e.g. only a drop kick may be used to re-start from the 22m line.

Kicking from your hands

Punt

The critical factor in 'punting' a rugby ball is not merely the speed of the kicking leg but also the force that your foot imparts to the ball. This force results from the combination of leg speed and the manner in which your foot strikes the ball. It is essential therefore that you carefully control the placement of the ball onto the most effective part of that foot. Contrary to popular belief, this is not across the laces of your boot, because contact here causes your foot to give slightly, resulting in a loss of power. The best contact point is higher on your extended ankle, the hard bridge of your foot.

The angles at which you strike the ball in relation to the ground and in relation to the line of kick are also important. For maximum distance you should strike the ball at an angle of approximately 45 degrees to the

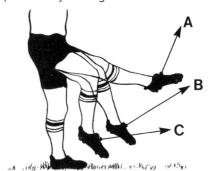

A **High up and under.** *B* **Long touch-kick.** *C* **Low grub-kick**

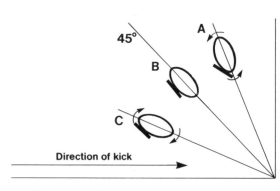

Direction of kick

A **High up and under.** *B* **Optimum angle for maximum distance.** *C* **Rolling kick to touch**

vertical. If the angle is less, you will strike the point of the ball nearest to you and if the angle is greater than 45 degrees you will strike the point furthest from you. These point-first

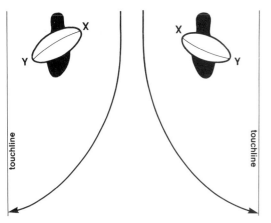

Right and left screw-kick to touch. Note how the ball is angled across the kicking foot. *X* **Top point of ball.** *Y* **Bottom point of ball**

contacts give an end-over-end flight and result in a considerable loss of distance. However, often this is desirable if you are trying a long, rolling kick for touch, a short grub kick into space or a high up-and-under.

Putting spin on the ball (the screw kick) gives greater distance and can cause the ball to swerve in flight. Spin is imparted by kicking the ball at its centre when it is lying at an angle across the line of your foot. It is a much surer method than trying to cut your foot across the ball as you kick.

Two other factors must be appreciated. First, your non-kicking leg must provide a firm support base for your kick. The longer the kick attempted, the firmer the base must be and you must recognise the need to steady yourself if running prior to kicking. Second, your kicking leg must be accelerating as your foot strikes the ball, and a full follow-through is necessary. If there is little or no follow-through, it can be assumed that your foot was slowing down on contact, with a resultant loss of power.

Carefully control placing the ball onto your foot

Your non-kicking leg must provide a firm base

Low diagonal kick and grub kick

The basic principles of these kicks are the same as those for punting. The only difference is the height and angle at which you strike the ball and the position of your foot in relation to your knee.

Short chip kick

Again the basic principles are the same, but in this kick you strike the ball somewhere between points A and B (see illustration, p. 22 (middle of second column)), and your ankle should be flexed with your toes turned up.

Short chip kick behind the defence

Straight line place kick

Kicking the ball from the ground

Place kicking

The place kick is only used for attempts at goal and for re-starts.

The two techniques of place kicking are:

1. the straight-line method
2. the round-the-corner method.

In the first method the ball is struck with the toe of your boot, swinging your kicking leg straight along the line of the kick. In the second method you strike the ball with the top of your foot along the line of your big toe, and your kicking leg swings in an arc across and through the line of the kick.

Success is the only criterion in deciding which technique to use. Both have advantages and drawbacks. On a wet day there is an obvious advantage in using the round-the-corner method, as a greater area of foot strikes the ball than with the straight-line method.

The key principles of both techniques are:

1. take an appropriate run
2. provide a stable base with your non-kicking leg
3. watch the ball until the moment of impact
4. follow through.

Accuracy and consistency are your most important objectives and, although you will never achieve 100 per cent success, the development of a sound technique is essential if good results are to be obtained.

Straight-line right-foot kick

Place the ball carefully: upright; or top point angled slightly towards you; or top point angled heavily away from you, so that the bottom point is presented as a target. Visualise the line of flight of the ball to the target and move back directly along that line to the required distance.

Approach on the same line in a relatively slow and relaxed manner, keeping your eyes on the ball. A fast run-up will not necessarily add power to your kick. Make a long last stride, placing your left foot about 25cm (10in) behind and 15cm (6in) to the side of the ball.

Round-the-corner method

kicking foot

Round-the-corner place kick

Swing powerfully with your right leg, keeping your ankle rigidly flexed to strike the ball with the toe of your boot. The contact point will depend upon the ball position: if the ball is upright or angled towards you, impact should be just below the centre of the ball. If the ball is angled away, your toe should strike exactly on the bottom point of the ball.

Think of swinging your foot through and beyond the ball. Try to maintain contact for as long as possible. Use your arms to balance and try to recover your right foot down beside your left in a normal standing position.

Round-the-corner right-foot kick

Place the ball carefully upright. Visualise the line of flight to the target and go back along that line to the start of your approach run.

Move two paces to your left, then approach on a slight arc from the left of the ball in a

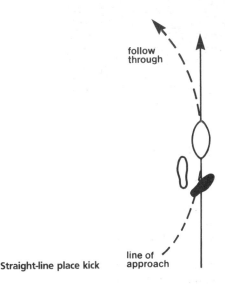

follow through

Straight-line place kick **line of approach**

slow, relaxed run. Keep your eyes on the ball. Make a long last stride, placing your left foot about 25cm (10in) behind and 15cm (6in) to the side of the ball. Push your left hip forwards into this stride.

Swing powerfully to hit the ball just below its centre across the top of your foot. Your foot must be tensed and extended. Swing through

25

and beyond the ball, keeping your foot going towards the target for as long as possible. Use your arms to balance and try to recover your right foot down beside your left to a normal standing position.

Drop kicking

The technique of drop kicking is virtually identical to that of the round-the-corner place kick except that:

1. you move forwards to kick, carrying the ball
2. as you make your long last stride, you drop the ball vertically to a point 25cm (10in) in front of and 15cm (6in) to the right of your left foot
3. contact is made just as the ball hits the ground.

Controlled dropping of the ball and timing of your kick are the critical factors, and they require constant practice.
N.B. The distances expressed are given as a guide only. You are not expected to take a measure onto the field!

Punting faults

Fault
1. Lack of power, no distance.
2. You are unable to screw kick.
3. You are unable to roll kick.
4. You are unable to chip kick.

Probable cause
1. Your foot is not accelerating through the ball. There is no follow-through. The point of contact is not in the centre of the ball. The kicking foot is not extended and tense. Contact is on the laces of the boot. The non-kicking foot is not providing a firm base.
2. You have the wrong contact point on the ball. The ball is wrongly angled across your foot.
3. The contact point is too high in relation to the ground. Your knee is not bent over the ball on impact. The angle of the ball is 45 degrees or more to the vertical on contact.

4. You are running too fast, and therefore have no firm base. The contact point is too low in relation to the ground. The kick is not made with a flexed foot.

Straight-line right-foot place kicking faults

Fault
All faults.

Probable cause
Almost all faults are caused by not striking the ball exactly in the centre of the target area with a firm, flexed foot. The target area is relatively small and there is little margin for error. The reasons for not striking the centre are usually:

1. not watching the ball up to impact
2. wrong placement of the non-kicking foot
3. not swinging the kicking leg through the ball along the line to the target.

Round-the-corner kicking faults

Fault
1. The ball is driven low.
2. The ball swings left of the target.
3. The ball is pushed to the right of the target.
4. Lack of power.

Probable cause
1. The point of contact is too high on the ball. The non-kicking foot is too near the ball.
2. The kicking foot is on the right of the line through the ball at impact. The non-kicking foot is too far behind the ball, or not far enough to the left of the ball.
3. The kicking foot is to the left of the line through the ball at impact. The non-kicking foot is not far enough behind the ball, or is too far to the left of the ball.
4. The point of contact is too low on the ball. The kicking foot is not accelerating at impact. The non-kicking foot is too far behind the ball. The last stride is too long.

Drop kicking faults

Fault
All faults.

Probable cause
The faults are much the same as those for round-the-corner place kicks and for the same reasons. The main additional causes of error are:

1. poor dropping of the ball
2. poor coordination of this and the kicking action
3. not watching the ball until impact.

Contact

Rugby is a physical contact sport and part of the pleasure of the game is in the physical challenge it sets. Courage and determination are essential factors in all contact situations but sound techniques are also necessary in order for you to enjoy contact safely. During a game you will come into contact with your opponents, your team-mates and the ground. The basis of all contact techniques is a satisfactory level of fitness, particularly strength, to enable you to withstand these physical encounters.

The general contact techniques applicable to all players are those involved in making and taking tackles. Specific techniques such as scrummaging and line-out support are dealt with in the section on unit skills.

Tackling

There are many ways of tackling, and no single technique is appropriate for every situation. Your tackling objective should determine the method you use. There are two basic objectives:

1. to stop the opponent who is carrying the ball
2. to regain possession of the ball.

Ideally, every tackle should aim to achieve both objectives but circumstances, including your opponent's ability, often make this difficult. It is generally far better to stop the player at least, rather than go for body and ball and get neither of them.

The key principles of tackling are as follows.

1. Move into a good position – tackling is relatively easy if you can get your opponent to go where you want him.

Contact practice

Grasp your opponent firmly

2. Tackle from a firm base, in order to exert force. If you were trying to push a car you would not try to do it standing on one leg or by taking a flying leap at it.
3. Unbalance your opponent; he will be trying to maintain a firm base to resist your tackle.
4. Grasp your opponent firmly – it is not always enough just to knock him off balance. He may recover and continue and, even if he falls down, he is not 'tackled' according to the laws and can get up or play the ball.
5. Grasp the ball if possible – it is not always enough just to tackle the opponent. Near your own goal-line a perfect body-only tackle may not be enough to prevent a try from being scored, and many tactics revolve around attackers committing defenders to a tackle but keeping the ball available for support players.
6. Keep your eyes open.

You can tackle an opponent from the side, rear or front, as outlined below.

Side tackle

When and why: The ball-carrier is running across your line of approach.

How: Drive in hard to unbalance the opponent by hitting him with your shoulder. Put your head behind him and your arms around him. Try to grasp your own hands and pull strongly. Extend your legs as you pull. Your contact point will be either just above knee height or, if you go for the ball as well, just above hip height.

Rear tackle

When and why: The ball-carrier is running away from you.

How: Make shoulder contact just below his buttocks (or just above his hips if you are going for the ball). Encircle his legs with your arms, pull and hang on. Providing you can stop his legs, his momentum will bring him down.

When and why: The ball-carrier is standing facing away from you.

How: Make shoulder contact just above hip height. Encircle him with your arms and try to get one hand on the ball. If your shoulder contact does not knock him down, you must pull strongly with your arms, twist and throw him down sideways.

Side tackle

Rear tackle

Front tackle

When and why: The ball-carrier is coming directly towards you.

How: If he has momentum, crouch to establish a firm base and aim to make shoulder contact just above hip height. Grasp him with both arms and hang on. He will almost certainly turn one shoulder into your tackle, which will help you to smother the ball with your arms. His momentum will cause him to fall over you and, as he unbalances, twist him strongly so that you fall on top of him.

Front tackle

When and why: The ball-carrier is facing you but with little or no momentum.

How: Drive into him hard and try to knock him backwards. Good shoulder contact just above hip height is important. Use your arms as above.

Ankle tap

When and why: The ball-carrier is running across and/or away from you and you are unable to get close enough to make a normal tackle.

How: This is a desperate tackle. Knock your opponent's rear nearside leg sideways across and behind his leading leg so that he effectively trips over his own feet. You must try to catch this rear leg just as it is fully extended.

Ankle tap

Overcoming a hand-off

When and why: When you are tackling from the side against an opponent with an effective hand-off.

How: If you are approaching from the right to tackle with your left shoulder, knock down his outstretched arm with your right forearm. Drive in with your left shoulder and arm as for a high smother side tackle. (You must be close to your opponent to be able to do this effectively.) If you are stretched to make the tackle, try to knock down his arm, then hang on to it and try to pull him down. Although not elegant, it can be very effective.

Overcoming the hand-off

Resisting and taking tackles

In resisting tackles, the key principles are similar to those involved in making them:

1. maintain a firm base
2. try to unbalance your opponent
3. keep your legs working
4. protect the ball.

Apart from the evasive techniques described in the section on running, there are two basic contact methods of resisting a tackle: shoulder dip and hand-off.

There are times, however, when you will have to take a tackle and concentrate on passing on the ball or making it available for your support players. On these occasions, try to take the tackle on your terms, positioning your body to make it harder for the tackler and easier for yourself. Try to meet the tackle with your hip and keep the ball in two hands, well away from the tackle area.

As you fall, twist your body so that you hit the ground across a broad area to absorb the impact. If the tackle is from the front, wrap yourself round your opponent to make it easier to pass the ball to a supporter.

Shoulder dip

When and why: Normally when you are bigger than your opponent and his approach is mainly from the front.

How: Try to unbalance your opponent with a slight change of direction. Hold the ball in your hand and arm further from the tackler. Check your forward momentum as the tackle is made and compress your body by lowering your leading shoulder and elbow towards your hip. Try to do this by going straight down. If you lean too far forwards, you will simply fall over the tackler.

If you succeed in knocking him off balance, straighten and accelerate away. If he stops you, fight to stay on your feet and make the ball available for your supporter.

Hand-off

When and why: A tackler is approaching from the side and you are isolated from support. It is most effective when the tackler is stretched to reach you or is coming in high, rather timidly and with his chest leading.

How: Hold the ball in your hand and arm

Keep the ball available in contact

further from the tackler. As your opponent commits himself to the tackle, extend your free arm and lock rigidly at the elbow. If he is coming in low, aim for his head and try to push him down. As you do so, move your hips away and recover your arm so he cannot grab it. If he comes in high, aim for his face or chest and simply try to check him as you push yourself away. This must be a short, sharp jab so that he cannot grab your arm.

An effective hand-off

Side tackle faults

Fault
1. Your opponent runs past you and you completely fail to make contact despite a despairing dive.
2. Your opponent runs through or out of your tackle.
3. You are easily handed off.
4. Your opponent beats you easily with a swerve or side-step.

Probable cause
1. Poor positioning and decision making. Unless you are hopelessly beaten for pace you must not commit yourself to the tackle until you are close enough to make firm shoulder contact. Lack of determination.
2. You are using your arms only and not driving in with your shoulder to unbalance him. You are not making your tackle from a firm base. Power comes through your legs in contact with the ground.
3. You are tackling too high with your body upright – a very ineffective driving position. You are tackling too low with your head down and diving off the ground before you make shoulder contact.
4. Poor positioning – you should aim to get your opponent to go where you want him. You are failing to approach the tackle under control. You should be able to accelerate into your tackle.

Poor tackling positions

Rear tackle faults

Fault
1. The tackle is missed completely.
2. Your opponent steps out of your tackle.

Probable cause
1. You are beaten for pace. You are committing yourself too soon – it is easy to misjudge distance when your opponent is moving away from you. Keep your feet on the ground and moving until you make contact and get your arms beyond your opponent.
2. You are not grasping firmly with your arms right around your opponent. You are tackling too low, and are likely to get a kick in the teeth for your trouble.

Front tackle faults

Fault
1. Your opponent runs 'through' your tackle.
2. You bounce off your opponent.

Probable cause
1. You are failing to get your shoulder in front of him. You are not making your tackle from a firm base.
2. You are not making your tackle from a firm base. You are not giving with your opponent's momentum. You lack determination.

Unit and positional skills

The scrum

Importance and objectives

The ability of a team to scrummage effectively is one of the most important aspects of rugby. On your own put-in this means winning your own ball every time with the scrum moving forwards or, at worst, rock solid. On your opponents' put-in it means driving them backwards to disrupt their possession and occasionally winning the ball against the head.

Recent analysis of matches has indicated that there is an average of 30 scrums in a game and that 90 per cent of these last for 20 seconds or longer. It is also estimated that out of the 80 minutes allowed for a match, the ball is actually in play for only about 27 minutes. Scrummaging therefore takes up a large proportion of the total playing time in a game of rugby, and is an important area of play. It makes great physical demands on the players involved and affects their ability to perform their other tasks in line-outs, rucks and mauls, in support of attacks, and in defence.

Good scrummaging can give an enormous boost to the morale of a team and can be extremely damaging to the opposition, and this impact does not just apply to the forwards. If your are a back, it certainly gives you confidence to know that you are going to win good possession from every scrum on your own put-in, and it is equally heartening to see your opponents in retreat and disarray on their ball. The benefits of dominant scrummaging are also important tactically. Guaranteeing good possession from each of your put-ins enables your team to dictate the pattern of play. It provides an excellent platform from which to initiate attacks and makes playing out of

defensive positions relatively easy, as the opposition forwards are tied down in the scrum and their backs are stationary or retreating.

It also helps you to achieve continuity, as your players will normally be going forwards to breakdowns and will thus have a decided advantage. Conversely, by exerting great pressure on your opponents on their ball, you will limit their effectiveness in attack and defence. In attack they will be operating from a standing start at best, and in defence they will have to deal with untidy possession with your players bearing down on them.

Effective scrummaging

You must have a positive attitude towards scrummaging and appreciate its importance and objectives. Commitment, concentration and control are the elements upon which your attitude must be based, together with unity and strength.

You must be totally committed to the task in hand and to the cause of your team at every scrum. Scrummaging consistently demands great physical effort and there is no room for slackers or for players who occasionally use a scrum as an opportunity to take a breather. Physical effort alone is not enough, however, and mental application through intense concentration is also required.

You must always be aware of the tactical implications of each and every scrum and ensure that you carry out your individual responsibilities efficiently.

Control is the third key element and applies to physical and mental efforts. Loss of self-control by any player in the face of opposition pressure or intimidation, or through sheer frustration, can completely ruin the collective effort of the scrummage. Similarly, a powerful scrum can be wasted due to loss of control of the ball as it is released to your scrum-half.

Unity

Good scrummaging is essentially a unit activity involving all eight forwards. Each player must not only fulfil a specific individual role but must also contribute to the effectiveness of the scrum as a whole. Working as a unit is a vital aspect of good forward play throughout the game, but it is particularly important in the scrum.

Front-row players, especially prop forwards, often seem to forget this as they become immersed in an intensely personal head-to-head confrontation with their opposite numbers. The ability to harness the power and technique of eight individuals into a dynamic, cohesive force is the real secret of successful scrummaging.

Strength

Strength is another important factor. All forwards must be strong enough to play their part in the scrum. They must be strong enough to get into and hold the required body positions, to withstand intense discomfort and physical pressure, and to generate explosive power when necessary. A great deal of individual scrummaging technique is totally dependent on this strength factor.

Scrummage mechanics

With a positive, aggressive attitude, unity and strength, a pack of forwards can generate tremendous power, but unless that force is directed in the right way, much of their effort may be wasted. A pack also has to be able to resist force being applied by the opposition and in both instances the application of sound mechanical techniques is essential.

Individual considerations

Power comes from your legs. To produce this power your legs must be bent at the knee to

start with. For example, try jumping into the air from a standing position without bending your knees. If you bend your knees too far, however, although you have a greater potential length of drive, it takes a lot of effort to start the movement and the result is inevitably slower than a drive over a short distance. As you will normally want a strong, fast drive or 'snap shove' in scrummaging, a compromise is necessary. Try bounding into the air off two feet from a variety of bent-knee positions until you appreciate the point. Although there will be slight variations according to individual positions in the scrum, a good general rule is that your pushing thigh should be vertical.

Drive starts from your feet. This may sound obvious but many players appear to forget this simple fact. Your feet must be in firm contact with the ground. Some players splay their feet sideways, which gives good stud contact but puts quite a strain on their knee ligaments. Most top-class forwards pack down with their feet pointing forwards and their knees and ankles flexed in line.

You must drive off a stable base. A wide base provides this stability, so get your feet as wide apart as you can without becoming too

Keep pushing your thigh vertical

Hips should be below shoulders

uncomfortable or interfering with your colleagues in the scrum.

The power is transmitted through your spine. Keep your spine in line with the direction of shove. Remember, your neck is part of your spine, so keep your head up (push your jaw forwards) and keep your hips slightly below your shoulders. Your back should not be flat but slightly depressed in the middle. When you start to drive it is important to maintain this position by pressing your hips towards the ground. Generally speaking, the lower you can get (in line), the more effective your drive will be.

The seven-man scrum

As your hooker has to concentrate on striking for the ball on your own put-in, only seven forwards will be concerned with shoving. In these seven-man scrums all the power goes through the props. They must keep their spines in line with the direction of shove in order to transmit this power to your opponents. A prop who bores in may well swing out; he will also disrupt the lock behind him and consequently reduce the effectiveness of his own pack's forward drive.

Props must provide a stable platform for the locks to shove against. The locks themselves

must bind tightly together at hip level to produce a concerted effort and to provide a firm link through which the No. 8 can contribute to the drive. The 3–4–1 formation is generally accepted as the most efficient method of packing. Flankers should pack at an angle to help keep their props' hips in line as the scrum engages. If the ball is secured and a further drive is called for, the flankers should move in so that they are shoving more directly in line.

The eight-man scrum

When the opposition are putting the ball in and your hooker is not striking against the head, you can have all eight forwards contributing to the shove. In an eight-man scrum the power goes through the entire front row and your hooker should adopt a similar position to that of his props. If he has a long enough back he should get his hips and feet in line with theirs. Some hookers adopt the underarm method of binding to help them get into this position.

With the front row packing in line, your locks will now have two hips to push against and they should bind tightly at shoulder level to maximise their concerted effort. Your flankers should pull themselves in on the locks and shove directly behind the props.

Binding

For a compact, solid scrum, good tight binding of the players onto each other is essential. Forwards usually make great efforts through their legs and bodies in a scrummage but often neglect the use of their arms and particularly their hands. Simply by really squeezing together and gripping each other, you can exert pressure on your opponents.

Ball channels and foot positions

The one important factor that must never be forgotten, of course, is the ball. The prime objective of the scrummage is to provide good possession. To win such possession the ball has to be directed from the tunnel between the two

Direction of shove

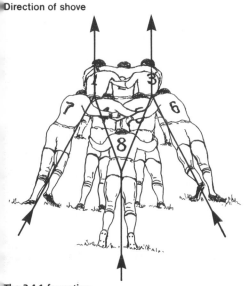

The 3-4-1 formation

A solid, compact scrum

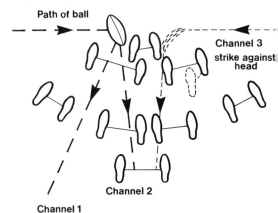

Below **Foot positions needed to produce the three main ball channels**

packs to a point somewhere behind this where it can be safely collected and distributed. Players must therefore position their feet so that they can not only shove effectively, but also leave a passage or channel for the ball to pass through. Three main ball channels are normally required and the diagram illustrates the foot positions needed to produce these.

Channel 1 ball passes between the legs of the left prop and emerges from the scrum between the left flanker and left hook. The ball tends to come out very quickly from this channel. It can be useful when your pack is under pressure and cannot afford to spend too much energy-sapping time down in a scrum, but the lack of control can cause problems for your scrum-half.

Channel 2 ball normally passes through the legs of the left prop and the left lock, to the feet of the No. 8. From this position, the ball can be released to the scrum-half; picked up by

the No. 8; controlled and driven forwards; or taken sideways and forwards in a wheel. A good Channel 2 ball therefore provides many options and is the sort of possession that provides the greatest control.

It does, however, require more skill at hooker than Channel 1 and your pack should preferably be going forwards. Channel 1 ball can often be converted into Channel 2 if the left flanker packs closer to the left lock and directs the ball across to the No. 8, and this is the compromise you should try for if your hooker cannot achieve a deep strike.

Channel 3 is the path followed by the ball on a strike against the head. The ball should normally pass between your hooker's right foot and the right prop's left foot (which will have been drawn back from its usual position). It will then pass between the legs of the right lock to the feet of your No. 8. Here the options are the same as those for Channel 2 ball, except that,

Channel 1 strike

Organisation starts before the front row engages

when releasing the ball to your scrum-half, the No. 8 will leave it outside his left foot, away from the opposing scrum-half.

Snap shove

Snap shove vividly describes the concerted effort a pack must be able to produce when required. It is a short, sharp, explosive drive and the key elements are organisation, good body and foot positions, and timing.

Organisation must start before the scrum goes down. Your front row and flankers must get into position quickly and the front row must never engage the opposition unless they can see and feel the heads of their locks and flankers in place. You should then drive into the opposition aggressively with one step only: left prop, left foot forwards; hooker and right prop, right feet forwards. Keep your feet firmly in position, because any shuffling about at this stage will reduce the effectiveness.

The front row must also aim to go in very low and then lift slightly on contact. This will put you in a lower and more effective position than your opponents. Depending on the objectives of the particular scrum, any binding adjustment must be completed before engaging the opposition.

Once in a sound position, the following sequence of action should be followed by all players exactly together.

1. Squeeze – tighten your bind by pulling with your arms and gripping with your hands to build up the pressure.
2. Press – lower your knees slowly 15cm (10in) towards the ground, keeping your pushing thigh vertical. This lowers the whole scrum, adds to the pressure, and effectively cocks the trigger ready for the shove.
3. Drive – force your hips down towards the ground and powerfully straighten your legs at the knee. The downward hip movement is very important to ensure that the drive goes forwards and not upwards.
4. Recover – if sufficient forward momentum is achieved, bring your feet quickly forwards to get your pushing thighs vertical again. A secondary drive may be necessary. Keep your hips low when recovering and do not relax your arm-and-hand bind.

Good timing is important, and much will depend on the objectives of each scrum. If the shove is to help your hooker win his own ball, the drive must coincide with the put-in. Communication is necessary to help the timing. Audible signals are easy to react to but also forewarn the opposition, so a visual cue is likely to be effective. One method is for the squeeze and press to begin when your scrum-half shows the ball below his knees, and to drive as the ball comes in.

If a secondary drive is needed, to help channel the ball if it gets stuck or to go for a push-over try, this can be called for by your No. 8 if it is not already a matter of habit. As soon as the ball is struck, your hooker should get his feet back into a pushing position. Having recovered their feet from the initial drive everyone then goes through the sequence again: squeeze, press, drive and recover.

When the snap shove is against your opponents' put-in, the front row should go in even more aggressively and try to rock the opposition one pace backwards or take a step to the right immediately on contact. This causes your opponents to re-adjust their foot positions and disrupts their timing and organisation. The front row should also go in even lower than usual but must ensure that in doing so, they bend from the knees, not just from the waist, otherwise the scrum may collapse. Holding the scrum very low makes it difficult for the opposing hooker to strike for the ball. The sequence leading to the drive is the same as before but the timing is slightly different. As your opponents will be making their effort as the ball is put in, it is often better just to hold them at this moment and make your biggest effort immediately after their hooker strikes the ball.

If you are slightly stronger in the scrum than they are, however, go for your snap shove on the put-in. Your flanker on the put-in side should call the timing loudly as he can see the opposing scrum-half clearly.

Locking the scrum

If you are faced with heavier and stronger opponents, it may be futile to attempt to snap shove on your own ball, and you should settle for not going backwards. Locking the scrum is simply a way of making your body as rigid as possible to withstand the drive of your opponents. To do this, you must splay your feet to reduce ankle flexion and get a firm contact with the ground, and keep your legs straight at the knee and almost straight at your hips. You must also press down hard towards the ground with your hips.

The flankers, locks and No. 8 are chiefly responsible for locking. Props cannot quite get into the locked position as they have to

You do not want the scrum to collapse

maintain a pushing platform at hip level. Too low here and the lock forwards will slide up over their backs. The props must therefore strive to keep their shoulders and hips in line, heads up and spines straight. The hooker can help by driving forwards off his left leg as he strikes and then trying to keep that leg braced instead of collapsing, as is so often the case. If possible the players on the right-hand side of the scrum should try to get lower than the rest to try to counteract the natural wheeling movement that may occur when the opposition drives.

In a locked scrum the ball is often struck through Channel 1, as the hooker is usually under pressure. Even if he manages to hit Channel 2, the ball may get stuck before it reaches your No. 8. If this happens, the locked scrum must be transformed into a forward drive. This is not easy and requires careful timing. If you have successfully managed to hold your opponents' first drive, they will probably relax momentarily. This is the time to strike back, but first the trigger must be cocked.

Tighten your binding, give a little against their weight and let them push your knees into the vertical thigh position, then explode forwards with a strong hip press and leg drive. It is essential that everyone acts together, otherwise you will find yourselves slithering backwards. Constant practice is the key to success.

The wheeling scrum

Wheeling the scrum has become one of the most destructive tactics in the game. It can be used effectively as an attacking ploy and an aid to your scrum-half in getting the ball away from the right-hand side of the field, but is is most commonly used to disrupt your opponents on their put-in.

Because of the way the players pack down, and the mechanics of the 3–4–1 formation, scrums usually wheel in a clockwise direction. It is possible to wheel the other way but it is much more difficult and usually only possible when the wheeling team is much stronger and heavier than their opponents.

The easiest way to start a wheel is for the left prop, lock and No. 8 to drive forwards through their left shoulders with the right prop, lock and flanker holding their positions. The left flanker should push directly behind his prop. The wheel is most effective if preceded by a powerful eight-man shove. If you are using the wheel it is important that you can control it and are organised to gain advantage from it.

If you are wheeling your opponents on their ball, do not turn them through more than 90 degrees, as this simply stops play.

The controlled wheel is most effective at scrums near your right touch-line, as it severely limits your opponents' attacking options. During most wheels, there is a pause when the wheel loses its initial impetus. This is a good time to put in another powerful snap shove, which can wreak further havoc on your opponents' side.

Counters to the wheel

It is virtually impossible to stop a wheel if your opponents are determined to turn the scrum. There are, however, a number of counter-measures you can take to make the best of the situation:

1. Go for a quick strike out of Channel 1 if your hooker and scrum-half are good enough.
2. Before the scrum turns through 45 degrees, your No. 8 can pick up and feed your scrum-half standing back, or he can pick up and drive into the opposition scrum-half with support from your right-hand flanker. If they

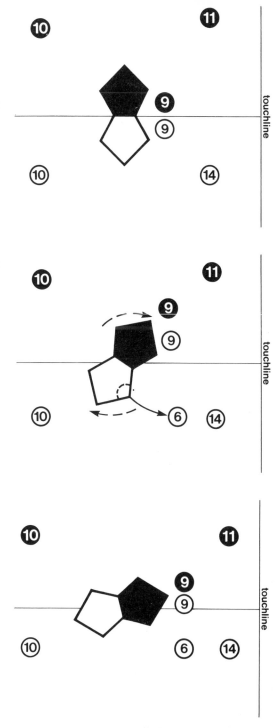

A wheel by White near the right-hand touchline

39

can drive beyond the gain line and stay on their feet, you may be able to sustain the drive with good support and produce good ball from any subsequent ruck or maul. At worst you should be able to force another scrummage with your put-in.

3. If the wheel quickly loses its initial impetus and you still have control of the ball, put in a powerful counter-shove. Your opponents will probably have had at least one player detached and are likely to be caught off guard.

All these measures should be practised regularly so that you can reduce the effects on your possession of your opponents' disruptive wheeling tactics.

The scrum – individual responsibilities

A sound front row is essential for effective scrummaging. Strength, allied to technique, is the most important requirement for front-row forwards, particularly props. Props not only transmit the power of their own scrum but also act as the buffers receiving directly the force of the opposition. They must, therefore, be able to withstand intense compression.

Left prop

The left, or loose-head, prop is the key player in the scrum. On your own ball you have to ensure that your hooker has a clear sight of the ball and has enough height to be able to strike for it with his right foot. To do this, you have to resist the downward pressure exerted by your immediate opponent and yet still be in a position to transmit the drive of your own scrum. You must therefore keep your shoulders parallel to the ground and your hips slightly below your shoulders. Force your head up under the opposing prop's breastbone and keep your spine in line with the direction of shove. You should not normally allow your head to slip sideways under your opponent's right armpit, though some well-known players, especially from New Zealand, have adopted this technique.

You should not try to follow the ball into the scrum but should adopt a wide stance with your left foot slightly ahead of your right. This not only gives you a firm base but keeps your right hip close to your hooker and helps him to strike the ball between your legs. Although having your feet well back would give you a more effective driving position, you must provide a platform for your lock forward to push against, so keep your buttocks fairly high and rock solid.

It is important that you scrummage with bent knees, and any raising or lowering in the front row must be controlled from your knees and not from your waist. If you lift from the waist only, you could dissipate your pack's shove, be exposed to your immediate opponent and give their hooker a good chance of striking for the ball. If you lower from the waist only, you will direct all your pack's force into the ground and probably cause the scrum to collapse.

It is also essential that you keep your right knee behind your hips. If your right thigh moves forwards, your lock will slide down and, due to the pressure from the other side, you are liable to be popped out of the top of the scrum. To hold these positions, it can be an advantage if you are short and stocky.

Binding at loose-head is also important. Your bind on the hooker should be according to his requirements. Most hookers like a tight contact at hip level but prefer to control the strength of arm bind themselves. If you bind too tightly on him with your right arm, it can limit his range of movement on his right side and affect his strike, so let him dictate where and how tightly you bind on him.

You must also bind on your immediate opponent with your left arm according to the laws, but within these, try to get your left hand well up on your opponent's back so that your left shoulder is high and firm. Keep your elbow out to hold this position and bear down onto your opponent with your right shoulder. You must avoid being twisted with your left shoulder down and right shoulder up. If you have to compromise, try to bind straight ahead onto the waistband of your opponent's shorts. This may cause your left elbow to drop down into your hooker's line of vision, so it is important that you lift it out of the way as the ball comes in.

Right prop

On the tight-head side you also have to be technically competent and very strong. Your main tasks on your own ball are to transmit the drive of your pack and be as disruptive as possible to the opposition. Your position is basically similar to that of the loose-head, though you may push your right leg a little further forwards, and you must bind with your right arm on your opponent in accordance with the laws. When binding on your hooker within the laws, he should again dictate the method and type of bind, but a strong left-arm pull from you can often help his striking action.

It is essential that you keep your buttocks up and in line for your lock to push on. If your hips move out, the right lock is likely to fall forwards into the gap between you and your hooker, and the whole scrum will be disrupted.

Hooker

Your most important job is to win your own ball and do so without unduly upsetting the rest of your scrum. Strength is essential but so also is suppleness, particularly at your hip and shoulder joints. Strength is needed because of the way you are pinned in the scrum with tremendous weight bearing down on your neck and shoulders. Suppleness is required because you have to bind firmly at shoulder level with your props, but still be able to time your foot strike to the ball and get there before your opponents.

The laws dictate that you must bind at or below your props' armpit level, but whether you go over or under their nearest shoulders to get there is a matter of individual choice.

It is generally agreed that the over-arm bind is the most effective on your own put-in. This not only gives a firm bind but puts you as near to the ball and the centre of the tunnel as possible. Some hookers occasionally bind with one arm under and one arm over. If you bind under on the left, this takes you away from any pressure from the opposing tight-head but also takes you slightly back from the centre. If you bind under on the right, it allows your right hip to drop nearer the ball but prevents you from exerting any pressure on the opposing hooker.

Whichever method you use, the most important and tightest bind must be on the side nearer the ball. This helps you to turn your hips towards the ball and makes possible an easier and faster strike.

Going into the scrum, you should first bind with your left prop, with his right hand firmly clenching your shirt at chest level or just above the waistband of your shorts. The tight-head will then bind over the arm of the loose-head, firmly anchoring his right elbow in place. As you engage your opponents, push your right shoulder forwards and keep your head close to your left prop, stepping in with your right foot as he moves forwards with his left. This immediately puts you in a position to strike.

Strike for the ball with your right leg. A left-foot strike may be quicker but it gives poor control and really needs the assistance of your left prop. A right-foot strike gives greater control and allows your prop to concentrate on his main task. The position you adopt in the scrum is limited by the laws. Both feet must be on the ground, must not be crossed and must be in a position for an effective forward shove. Virtually all your weight should be on your left leg, to keep your right leg relaxed and ready to strike. By pressing your head and upper body to the right you will be able to get your feet a little nearer the ball and ease the striking action.

When the ball comes in, you must react quickly. The strike should be a short kicking action to get beyond the fall, followed by a strong raking movement to direct the ball back through the left prop's legs. Control is important and the part of your foot that strikes the ball should vary according to the channel being used. For a Channel 1 strike you should hit the ball with the sole of your boot, but for a Channel 2 the contact will be more on the heel and you must try to drag the ball towards your No. 8.

Many hookers neglect to use their left leg to assist their strike. A powerful drive of this leg will extend your length of strike and make control easier. You should also recover your striking leg quickly so that you can then help the rest of your pack to resist your opponents' pressure or contribute to your forward drive.

Good communication with your scrum-half will help your timing of the strike. It is better for you, rather than the scrum-half, to decide when the ball should come in. Most hookers use a hand or finger signal with their left hand, but an alert opposing right flanker can often spot this. With practice you should be able to develop a reaction strike, going for the ball as soon as the scrum-half puts it in.

Striking for the ball against the head

If you go for the ball when your opponents put it in, your chances of winning it can be improved if all front-row players adjust their technique and positioning. It is helpful, therefore, if the decision to go for the ball is made before the scrum goes down.

Your left prop should try to put pressure on his opponent to try and weaken the support for their hooker. He must also push his hips towards the ball to give you, as hooker, more support, while at the same time maintaining his in-line position.

Your tight-head should try to drive under and lift his opponent to give you more freedom of movement and a better sight of the ball. He can also help you by following the ball into the scrum with his right foot. To be able to do this, however, he must move his left foot from its normal wide stance to a deeper position almost directly behind his right foot. This opens up a channel for the ball and enables the prop to take almost all his weight on his left leg. He must still try to keep his hips square so that the right lock has something to push against and he must not take his opponent too high, as this might reduce the effect of your pack's shove.

Many hookers change their binding when going for a strike against the head, usually by binding under on the left and over on the right. There are three main methods of striking, and in each case you should use your right foot, the foot nearer the ball. The most common method is the reflex strike, made with a swift kicking action from the knee, aiming to intercept the ball with the outside of your right foot. The right prop follows the ball in and it is trapped between you, then squeezed back down the ball channel.

A second method is for you to force your head and shoulders away from the ball and strike by quickly straightening your leg towards the ball to make contact with your heel. The assistance of your right prop is again required to direct the ball down the ball channel.

The third method requires a high degree of skill, speed of movement and flexibility in your hip joint. The strike is a kicking action aimed beyond the ball, with your toes turned out towards the mouth of the tunnel. You must then drag the ball back under control with the outside of your foot. If you are good enough you may not need any help from your tight-head prop.

Lock forwards

The locks are often referred to as the engine room or powerhouse of the scrum. As the name implies they are also largely responsible for holding the scrum together. To perform this dual role of generating power and locking the unit, you must have strong legs for the shove, strong backs and abdominal muscles to maintain a good body position, and very strong arms and shoulders to tie in the props and keep a tight bind on each other. There is little difference between the role of the left and right lock – indeed it is essential that you act as one. However, each of you may need to modify your technique slightly to compensate for the variable movements of your front-row players in different situations.

In the seven-man scrum, you should both transmit your power through your outside shoulders onto the inside buttock of your prop. The contact point is actually the niche where the prop's buttock joins his thigh. You should have little weight going onto your hooker, particularly on the right side.

In an eight-man shove, however, as the hooker should have his feet back in line, each lock should shove through both shoulders. Your shoulders must be parallel to the ground, with your spine in line with the direction of shove. Keep your head up and chin forwards to maintain a flat back, with your hips slightly higher than your shoulders. If the left prop has his right leg well across, it may be necessary for the left lock to put his head between the prop's legs. The normal position, however, is between the prop and the hooker.

The binding of locks on their props and on each other is extremely important. The most commonly used bind is between the prop's legs with your outside arm, grasping a good handful of shirt around the top of the prop's shorts. Some locks even reach to the collar of the prop's shirt. An alternative method is to wrap your arm around the prop's inside leg, grasping a handful of shorts around the hip pocket. It is really a matter of personal preference between prop and lock. It is important that the bind is really tight without interfering with the prop's function or upsetting the body position needed by the lock for an effective shove. Pushing your elbow forwards as far as possible will tighten the bind wherever you grip.

Locks must also bind on each other with their inside arms. At left lock you will usually find it better to bind under the armpit of your partner. This helps to push your left shoulder onto your prop and brings your right shoulder away from your hooker. On your own put-in you should grasp each other near to the top of your shorts. This also helps to keep your inside shoulder back from your hooker. When going for an eight-man shove, it is more effective if you bind at armpit level. You must grip and squeeze as tightly as possible and drive forwards with your arms as well as with your legs.

Keep your feet at least shoulder width apart to give good sideways stability. Your knees must be bent prior to pushing, with your thighs vertical. This will determine how far back you put your feet, which must be very firmly pressed into the ground. You will now be in a good position from which to squeeze, press and drive for a snap shove. On your put-in you must resist the temptation to lift your feet to guide the ball back to No. 8. If your hooker doesn't get a deep strike and you have to help, use your knees. You should be low enough. Try to drive forwards over the ball if it gets stuck or get the nearest flanker to give it a nudge.

Flankers

Flank forwards must be very good all-round players. You need the strength and skill of a lock and the speed and ball-handling ability of a centre. At a scrummage your first duty is to push. You are just as important to the effectiveness of the scrum as the locks are, so get down and work. Bind onto your nearest lock with your head in position on the prop's outside hip as the scrum goes down. Your normal head position should be to suit your prop, but you should be able to see into the tunnel and watch the ball throughout the scrum. Get your hips slightly higher than your shoulders to start with, unless you are locking the scrum right away. Your outside foot should be slightly ahead of the other. Try to keep your shoulders and hips parallel to the ground. It is very easy to drop your outside shoulder and twist your hips out of an effective pushing position.

The left flanker should pack at an angle as the scrum forms but, unless you are using Channel 1 ball, you should move in as the drive starts so that all the shove goes forwards.

Both flankers should bind firmly with the inside hand and arm at a place that suits their locks. When you pull on that arm to assist the drive, remember to pull yourself into your lock rather than pull him away from his partner. The left-hand flanker has some responsibility for channelling the ball and must be aware of which channel is being attempted. The right-hand flanker may have to call for the timing of the shove on your opponents' put-in and must also be ready to slide around the back to assist your No. 8 if you are being wheeled on your ball.

The secondary role of the flankers at the scrummage is defence close to the scrum when the opposition win the ball. The simplest organisation of this defence is that on the side the ball is put in, your scrum-half should tackle the first opponent with the ball while the flanker takes the second one. On the other side the flanker is responsible for the first opponent with the ball. When your opponents are putting the ball in, it is most likely that their attack will be on your left side of the scrum. It is most important that the left flanker always knows exactly where the ball is, particularly near your own line. If you lose sight of it you could be caught napping, so if you can't see the ball, come off the scrum about one metre wide and on the offside line.

If the scrum wheels, the left-hand flanker should stay on the scrum but the right flanker

Blind-side flanker poised to defend

will normally come off to a position one metre wide on the offside line.

When tackling, flankers must try to go forwards to meet the attackers and should always try to make body-and-ball tackles.

No. 8 forward

The No. 8 forward has to have the same physical attributes as the flankers, though he is usually taller, and is often used as a third line-out jumper. At the scrummage, your first job is to control the scrum and control the ball when Channel 2 is being used. You must push through both shoulders under the buttocks of

the inside legs of your locks, binding tightly at hip level around their outside legs. Don't try to bind through their legs, as this is a very unstable position.

Keep your hips above your shoulders, but keep your head up with your chin pushed forwards to ensure a good, flat back. With your thighs vertical, your feet will be well back in line, slightly outside shoulder width apart and firmly anchored to the ground. Hold your locks in strongly and make sure they keep pushing in line. When your hooker strikes the ball, you will have to drop your head to see it clearly. If the channel is right it should arrive quickly at your feet. Keep it there for a moment to ensure control. Then you have several options and can:

No. 8 has a key role

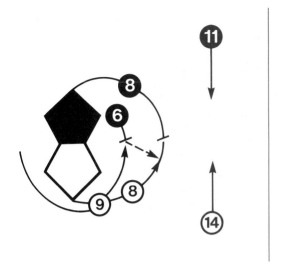

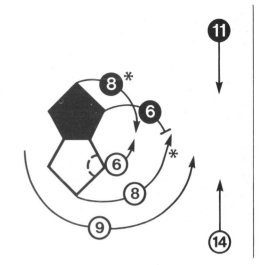

Back row defence (note decision points). *Left* Black no. 8 makes tackle outside his no. 6 *Right* Black no. 8 has to cover the inside gap

1. release the ball to your scrum-half by moving slightly to your left with your feet and hips so that the ball emerges away from the opposing scrum-half
2. in one movement withdraw your head, pick up the ball and give a short pass to your scrum-half
3. pick up the ball and drive forwards around the right-hand side of the scrum
4. call for a secondary drive and, as the scrum moves forwards, keep the ball under control at your feet
5. pick up the ball and drive around the left side of the scrum with support from your right flanker and scrum-half

6. break off flat and to the right, leaving the ball for your scrum-half to give you a short, fast pass so that you can attack the right side of the scrum.

Occasionally you can move to the left and pack between the left flanker and lock to control the ball in Channel 1. This can give you a better position to launch an attack to the left of the scrum, but it is not a strong scrummaging position and you need to have a dominant front five if this position is to be really effective. Good communication with your scrum-half is essential to ensure that you select the correct option at the right time.

The back row must work as a unit in defence

Your secondary role at the scrum is close defence in conjunction with your scrum-half and flankers. On the side the ball is put in you are responsible for the third opponent with the ball, and on the other side for the second one. Most attacks will be on your left. If the first tackle is made close you should move wide, but if your flanker takes his opponent wide, you must plug the gap on the inside.

The line-out

Importance and objectives

Statistically, the line-out is the most dominant single feature of Rugby Union and there are about 45 line-outs in every match. Line-outs are an important source of possession, and now have the same physical and psychological impact as scrums. A team that can dominate the line-outs can control a game.

Unlike scrums, however, where the odds are heavily in favour of the team putting in the ball, at a line-out each team has a reasonable chance of winning possession. Unfortunately this relative equality often results in an undignified and seemingly chaotic scramble for the ball. It is the team that can create order out of chaos that will be more successful at line-outs.

The essential element in producing good possession is control. Without control, the possession you win may be of more value to your opponents than it is to you, especially if they can force you into error and drive you back towards your own line.

You can win possession from line-outs in many ways. The ball can be caught and held by the jumper; passed or deflected off the top of the jump directly to your scrum-half; or passed or deflected to another player in the line-out. The ball can even be thrown right over the top to be gathered by a player not involved in the line-out.

The place in the line-out where the ball is initially won and from which it is then distributed will also vary according to the requirements of your team. If the line-out is near your own goal-line you may throw to your front jumper, expecting a low catch and

forward drive. If, however, you are in a good attacking position, your backs may well want the ball off the top of the jump direct to your scrum-half from the middle of the line.

There are many combinations of positioning and technique available to a skilful pack of forwards, and it is important that players select the technique appropriate to the type of possession required.

Whatever your objectives at a particular line-out might be, the key elements are:

1. the throw-in
2. jumping and handling
3. support
4. communication.

The throw-in

It has often been said that the most important player at a line-out is the one who throws the ball. No matter how good your other players are, unless the ball can be delivered to the desired place at the right height, speed and trajectory, most of the skilled effort of the jumpers and supporters will be wasted.

There are many ways in which the ball could be thrown in, but whatever method is used, the essential principles are as follows.

1. The thrower must be able to see his target jumper to ensure good visual communication between them.
2. The target jumper must be able to see the ball from the moment the thrower prepares to throw, so that he can time his jump.
3. The technique used must enable the thrower to vary the length, height, speed and trajectory of his throw without having to make an obvious adjustment to his basic starting position.
4. The ball must have a fairly stable flight through the air, not turning end over end, to assist the jumper's handling.
5. The technique must produce consistently accurate results. The end product is the sole justification of the means.

The one-handed spin (torpedo) throw

The technique best able to meet all these criteria is the one-handed spin or torpedo throw, and it is currently the most popular method in use. The main elements of this technique (applied to right-handers) are as follows.

Grip
Hold the ball near one end with your fingers spread on one side, and your fingertips gripping a seam to help your control. Your thumb should be on the other side, as wide as possible and pressing firmly to grip the ball.

Stance
Stand with your feet shoulder width apart a few centimetres back from the touch-line, facing down the centre of the line-out. At all times try to keep your hips parallel to the touch-line. Draw your right leg back to give a comfortable base but keep your toes pointing at the line-out. Hold the ball just above head height. A few centimetres up or down is a matter for personal preference. Lean back slightly from the waist. Your right elbow should be out to the side just in front of the line of your shoulders. Keep your left elbow shoulder high. If it drops, the throw will almost certainly go off line. Some players hold the ball in two hands until just before they start to throw to ensure that their left shoulder stays up.

Arm and hand action
To start your throw, take your right elbow back behind the original line of the shoulders in a smooth movement. This elbow then starts the actual throw, swinging forwards and leading the throwing hand. As you straighten your forearm towards your target, press the ball away with your fingers and try to follow through down the line of flight.

The speed at which you do this and the moment and angle of release will vary according to the length and type of throw you are attempting.

Constant practice is the key to consistently

Throw-in grip and stance

Practice makes perfect!

accurate results. If you have small hands, or the ball is wet, you may have to modify your grip on the ball. Try holding it in the middle rather than near one end, with your fingers and thumb spread on the same side so that the ball is cradled rather than gripped. You must use a short, very smooth, take-away but a long, exaggerated hand action. This push-type technique is still very accurate to control beyond that distance.

Remember, although it is common practice, it is not necessarily the hooker who throws in. Your thrower should be the best person for the job selected on his throwing ability, providing that he is not required for some other critical role at the line-out.

Jumping and handling

Jumping

The ability to get into the air is the first requirement of a line-out jumper, and jumping power is basically a matter of leg strength.

The key factors are that you must jump off both feet, your knees must be bent prior to jumping, and you should move into your take-off. You must experiment to find the right amount of knee bend and type of movement into take-off that gives you the best results. Ideally at take-off your feet should be about shoulder width apart, almost directly below your hips. Driving your arms and shoulders up towards the ball will assist your jump, but remember to start with your arms outside the line-out to avoid interference by the opposition.

Because an opponent will be jumping against you and contact is inevitable, it is essential that you jump aggressively towards the line of touch and into a strong position, otherwise it will be impossible to achieve the vital control of the ball. To ensure this, try to get your leading shoulder high, keeping your hips and shoulders parallel to the touch-line. Bent arms are less easily displaced than straight arms, but this will of course be determined to some extent by the height of the ball and the ability of your opponent.

Timing your jump is obviously important and this can only be perfected through regular

The ability to jump is important

Your starting position for a catch is also important

A brilliant two-handed catch at full stretch

Below **Interference can make a two-handed catch difficult**

practice with your thrower. You cannot expect to jump in the same manner at every line-out and be successful. You must be prepared to modify your technique to adapt to your opponents and if necessary to the referee's requirements, and you must have at least two standard variations. Basically, these will entail jumping forwards to take the ball in front of your opponent and, alternatively, feinting to go forwards but then taking a high, lobbed ball behind him.

Whether you are catching or deflecting, the key factor in achieving control is to stop the ball by getting at least one hand behind the ball along its line of flight.

Catching

In a line-out, catching simultaneously with two hands is difficult due to the amount of interference by the opposition. More height can be achieved if one hand leads, stops the ball and guides it down to your other hand. At the front of the line, jumping at No. 2, you can sometimes get your chest behind the ball if you jump early, forwards and across, and get your thrower to whack the ball into you, fast and low.

Whenever you do catch the ball, it is important to be thinking at once about the next phase of action. This will be either immediate distribution or bringing the ball down into a strong, protected position ready for distribution. As soon as your hands make contact with the ball, turn your shoulders and hips towards your scrum-half. If you are passing immediately, push the ball down to him, aiming at his chest; otherwise snap the ball down to waist height and hold it there firmly with your elbows bent and wide. Land with your feet well spread and drop into a crouch with your chin tucked in to your chest. You will now be in a strong position to resist pressure from your opponents and can provide a firm base on which your supporting players can build their protective screen.

A protective screen

Deflecting

The ability to catch the ball is invaluable as it gives you more options and keeps the opposing backs behind their 10m (11yd) offside line. Unless you are much bigger and better than

Two-handed deflection

your opponent, however, it is likely that you will often have to settle for merely getting a hand to the ball before he does, especially in the middle and at the tail of the line. If you have to deflect, you must still aim to win the ball with control.

The key factor is to 'play down the line' as you might do in cricket. Get your hand in line with the flight of the ball to stop it, then by turning your wrist and pushing with your fingers, guide the ball in the required direction. You may sometimes find it necessary to deflect with your outside arm, using your inside arm and shoulder to fend off obstructive attempts by your opponents.

The easiest deflection is back down the line of flight and, the more the deflection is angled back behind you, the greater is the skill required. In a normal seven-man line-out with the main jumpers at positions 2, 4 and 7, there are a number of possible targets for deflections. Your order of priority could be as follows.

No. 2 jumper
1. Deflect backwards to No. 4 from two hands going forwards.
2. Forwards to No. 1 from one hand going back and high.
3. Straight to scrum-half from two hands going forwards.
4. Back to No. 4 from one hand going forwards or back.
5. Forwards to your hooker, especially on your opponent's throw, from two hands going forwards.

No. 4 jumper

1. Straight to the scrum-half.
2. Forwards to No. 2.
3. Forwards to No. 1.
4. Back to No. 6.

No. 7 jumper

1. Straight to your scrum-half.
2. Forwards to Nos. 4 or 5, peeling from the line.
3. Back to Nos. 4 or 5, peeling from the line.

In wet weather or if your jumpers are under severe pressure from their opponents, it will be safer if all deflections are forwards to another player in the line-out.

The reasons for jumping at 2, 4 and 7 are as follows. At 2 you only have one opponent between you and the ball and can get good support from 1 and 3. Jumping at 4 gives good protection for your scrum-half and allows your fly-half to stand well beyond the length of the line-out. Jumping at 7 gives you great freedom of movement going backwards and ties down your opponent at the end of the line, as well as enabling your fly-half to get even further away.

These positions can be varied, however, according to the requirements of your team and individual preference and ability. You may sometimes find it helpful to group all your jumpers together at the front, middle or tail of the line-out. When your opponents throw in, it may cause them problems in adjusting their technique if you stand one place in front of their jumpers.

Always, the criterion is: does the method you use produce controlled possession that can be used effectively?

Support

At any particular line-out on your own throw there will be at least one main target jumper, so what is expected of the other players involved? Every player taking part in a line-out must think of himself as a potential ball gatherer, and also as a ball and scrum-half protector.

At many line-outs the ball does not arrive at or is not taken cleanly by the target jumper and so other players must be alert and ready to snap up this loose ball. Head up and eyes open looking for the ball are therefore key requirements. Once the ball is secured it must then be protected from the opposition so that it can be released under control to your scrum-half. To ensure this, your basic aim should be to build a wall between the ball and your opponents.

When the line-out starts, the laws demand that there must be spaces between your players. These spaces are holes in your wall and if they remain after the ball has been won, your opponents will pour through onto the ball and your scrum-half. The first priority is therefore to close these gaps as soon as the laws allow.

If the ball is thrown to No. 4 in the line, players behind him must quickly move forwards as he leaps and makes contact, and players in front must quickly move back. The line is thus compressed towards the ball and the holes are

A difficult one-handed deflection

You must not leave gaps for your opponents to pour through

Support for the jumper is vital

firmly closed by each of your players getting shoulder to shoulder, hip to hip and binding strongly on each other's shirts. Players at the ends must ensure that no opponents come around the sides, and you should keep your wall as high as possible to prevent opponents from reaching over to get at the ball.

Players on either side of the target jumper have a special responsibility to provide him with early protection. They must move quickly into position and, if possible, reach behind him to isolate him safely on your side of the wall. If the jumper is jumping forwards to the ball, it helps if the player behind jumps forwards with him.

Bad-ball situations

Many line-outs do not go according to plan, largely as a result of the obstructive tactics of the opposition. If the ball is not gathered cleanly and drops to the ground, your first priority is to secure it immediately. If your wall is soundly

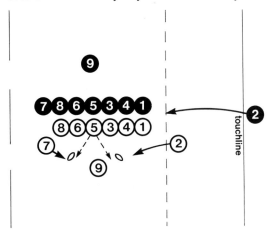

Sweeping up bad ball (note: this illustrates only one of many options)

The line-out must be a 'wall'

built, your scrum-half may be able to deal with the ball, but this is not always practical. An alternative is for another player to leave the line to fall on the ball, but if he comes from the middle, a hole will be left for your opponents to break through. It is probably better, therefore, to determine the approximate half-way point in the line, and any ball falling on the touch-line should be the responsibility of your thrower. A ball falling on the open-field side would be the responsibility of your last player in the line-out.

It is most important in these circumstances that the other players hold the wall for a second or two. If everyone rushes back towards the ball, your opponents will simply follow and put you under great pressure. Once the ball is secured, however, players must quickly get back in succession from the ends of the line to support the team-mate with the ball and try to drive him forwards before the ball is eventually released.

Communication

Successful line-out organisation depends upon each player knowing exactly what is being

attempted at every throw-in. Good communication is essential. The thrower must know where to throw the ball and what type of throw is required. Support players must also know these facts and how the jumper is going for the ball. Ideally, your opponents should not know any of these details.

Various methods of communicating can be used, but the key factor is to keep the signals as simple as possible to avoid confusion whilst at the same time disguising your intentions from the opposition. Regular practice and good decision making are vital. Your scrum-half is ideally placed to control the line-outs but the final choice of decision maker must depend upon the individual ability and personality of your players.

Line-out variations

The standard seven-man line-out may not always provide you with the quality possession you are seeking, particularly when your opponents are bigger and more skilful than you. You must therefore have alternatives at your disposal, and these are also useful simply to bring variety to your play and enhance your attacking options.

Whatever variation is attempted, however, the key factors remain the same: the throw, jumping and handling; support and communication. The objective also remains the same: to win good possession of the ball so that you can use it effectively.

The peel

A typical variation is the 'peel', usually around the tail of the line-out. The ball should be thrown long to No. 6 or No. 7 in the line, who deflects to support players running from the line, who in turn try to drive around and beyond the line-out. A throw to No. 6 maintains support behind that player but requires a very accurate throw. A throw to No. 7 gives more flexibility for both thrower and jumper and commits your opponents' last player, but it can make it difficult for the support players to get round the end of the line.

The easiest deflection is down towards the oncoming support runners, but it can be more effective to deflect the ball beyond the length of the line. This ensures that the ball gatherer will get beyond the length of the line before he is tackled. Any player can be used as the ball gatherer and preferably two or three players should be potential targets for the deflection.

My preference is to throw to No. 7 and for players Nos. 5, 4 and 2, in that order, to be the targets.

The second support runner has an important part to play in a peel. The first ball-carrier will quickly be tackled and the next support runner must be coming up on his outside shoulder to take a short pass and drive on beyond the defence.

Shortened lines

Reducing the number of players in your line is a common tactic. Even though it reduces the support for your jumpers, it also reduces the number of disruptive opponents and allows your jumpers more room to manoeuvre and your thrower greater flexibility. A major disadvantage is that the spaces away from the line-out are filled with players who would normally be involved, so it is important to consider what you are going to do with the ball once you have won it. Your basic aim must be to re-establish as much space as possible away from the line-out before you eventually release the ball to your backs.

Eight-man lines

Although the seven-man line is currently standard practice, reverting to eight players in the line

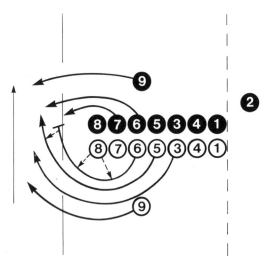

A peel at the back of the line (note the deflection options of the last player in the line)

A shortened line-out

can be effective. If your hooker rejoins the line you could use your wings to throw in the ball, but this means two different people are involved so it might be worth trying to use your scrum-half.

Ruck and maul

Importance and objectives

A ruck is formed when the ball is on the ground between one or more players from each team who are on their feet and in physical contact.

A maul is formed by one or more players from each team on their feet and in physical contact closing around another player who is carrying the ball.

Unlike the scrum and line-out, which are methods of re-starting play, the rucks and mauls occur during the course of play. At best, they are temporary interruptions to the progress of the ball, normally occurring when a ball-carrier is tackled or held by one or more opponents. The primary objective of each team at such times is to retain or regain possession, and a ruck or maul is simply the most effective collective technique available to players to ensure this.

All players must have a positive attitude to rucking and mauling and regard these situations as essential elements in maintaining the continuity of play.

Rucks and mauls have little value for their own sake. If your aim is to go forwards you should not seek to create artificial stoppages. Inevitably your opponents will check your progress but you must aim to minimise this and therefore be able to ruck or maul efficiently as required. This ability is required by all players, not just forwards, as a ruck or maul could develop on any part of the field.

Advantages and disadvantages

Advantages of rucking

1. A ruck is more likely than a maul to be dynamic and keep you going forwards.
2. It is capable of producing the ball very quickly in attacking situations.
3. It simplifies the role of support players.
4. It encourages dynamic tackling.
5. Backs can usually see the ball coming out and can organise their timing accordingly.

You must be able to ruck and maul

Disadvantages of rucking

1. Because the ball comes back on the ground you have few options available.
2. Many scrum-halves do not like to have to pick up and pass from the ground, especially in wet weather.
3. It may not have the control of a mauled ball.
4. It is difficult to ruck effectively if you are not going forwards.

Advantages of mauling

1. The ball is kept in your hands, therefore you should have good control.
2. You have more options than in a ruck as to what to do next.
3. Many scrum-halves prefer to receive the ball passed into their hands.
4. It is comparatively easy to practise.

Disadvantages of mauling

1. Mauls tend to be static.
2. In attack the ball is often produced slowly by being passed through many pairs of hands.
3. It requires good decision making by players.
4. It does not encourage dynamic tackling.

Both techniques have significant advantages and disadvantages, and there are no hard-and-fast rules about when to maul and when to ruck the ball. The main criterion is, does the technique used produce good possession that can be used effectively? The respective ability and physical attributes of your team and your opponents will largely determine which technique will be more successful in any particular match, but you will never be able to concentrate upon one to the complete exclusion of the other.

Ruck and maul are integral features of Rugby Union and your team must be proficient at both. If you need a framework, my general preference is to ruck when you are going forwards, driving the opposition back and producing a fast ball to continue the attack. When you have to go back to the ball, try to maul if you have a choice, containing your opponents and winning the ball with good control. An alternative framework is to concentrate on mauling when you are in possession, but when your opponents have the ball, knock them down and ruck over them.

Ruck-and-maul techniques

Although the specific techniques of rucking and mauling are different, the key factors of both are basically the same.

1. Support – the team that gets the most players to the point of breakdown first will have the better chance of winning the ball.
2. Go forwards – it is a basic objective of the game, and if you are going forwards your opponents will be retreating.

Good rucking provides a fast ball for the scrum-half to distribute

Good support is the key to successful play

***Below* The first support player makes the choice**

3. First player decides – the first support player to arrive on the scene must make a decision. He must either go for the ball (normally when it is held off the ground or if there are no opponents near) or drive the ball to provide a platform for the remaining support (when the ball is on the ground with opponents around).
4. Stay on your feet – all other support players must drive in parallel to the touch-line, aiming to go beyond the ball and driving the opposition backwards. They must stay on their feet. If you fall there will be neither a ruck nor a maul and the referee is likely to stop the game.
5. Ball wanted, not the whistle – the only point of rucking or mauling is to win the ball and maintain the continuity of the game.

Effective rucking

There are three specific methods of rucking.

Sink ruck

The sink ruck starts life as a maul or semi-maul, but if the ball channel back to the scrum-half is blocked for any reason or your opponents are getting their hands through onto the ball, the first support player should turn the maul into a ruck. If you are in this position, having taken the ball from the original ball-carrier, force yourself down to the ground away from the grasping hands of your opponents, release the ball and let your support players drive over you to leave

A sink ruck

the ball clear for your scrum-half to collect. It is important that the original ball-carrier stays on his feet to provide a platform for the rest of your players to drive against.

Post ruck

The post ruck also starts with the ball being carried into contact, but this time the decision to ruck rather than maul rests largely with the ball-carrier. If you are sure that you have support close behind you, put the ball down or post it back between your legs fractionally before you make contact. You must then stay on your feet, in contact with your opponent, to provide a platform for your supporters to drive onto. The first two support players should bind together early and drive in on either side of you. They must drive in very low, then lift up into the opposition to keep them on their feet. The next player drives into the hole between their hips with support on either side, with the next two into the holes behind these three.

This 2–3–2 formation gives a narrow spearhead and a tightly bound unit that is ideal for effective rucking. The outside players in the middle row must tie in any opposition fringe players at the edges of the ruck and sweep them away from the ball. All players must have their eyes open to see the ball and must keep their legs driving forwards with short, pumping steps. All support players must try to generate a horizontal impact, starting with their upper bodies parallel to the ground at least five metres from the ruck.

Foot ruck

The classic foot ruck starts when the ball is already on the ground, usually after a tackle, with the opposition already there. Your first two players to arrive must bind together early and drive in over the ball and any players lying on the ground. They must hit the opposition low and lift them up. If one player gets there first on his own, he must drive beyond the ball to provide the platform for these two. The rest of your support should drive over in a 2–3–2 formation as before.

A foot ruck

Effective mauling

The most important player in a maul is the original ball-carrier. If you are that player, the outcome of the maul largely depends upon your actions at the moment of contact. It is important that you make this initial contact on your terms so that you are in control of

The ball-carrier must fight to stay on his feet

Take the tackle on your terms

Practising the maul

The ball-carrier must make the ball available for his support players

subsequent events. Don't just succumb to a tackle.

Fight to stay on your feet by keeping your legs moving beneath you and try to keep your opponent more occupied with stopping you than with going for the ball. Hold the ball firmly, with fingers spread and elbows wide, so that it is away from your opponents but visible to your supporters. When it is taken from you by your first support player, use your arms to keep your immediate opponents on their feet.

If you are the first support player, look to see if a screen pass might be possible as you approach. If not, drive in directly behind the ball-carrier and try to knock him forwards. Get your nearer arm over the ball and, as other support players drive over and to either side of you, force the ball down and pull it into your hands. You should now have the ball in control and isolated from your opponents by at least three players.

If other opponents or further support players are slow to arrive, try to roll off and drive forwards with the ball. If the opposition are there in force, wait until your support builds a solid maul, then move the ball quickly to the back of that maul. You can then:

1. feed the ball to your scrum-half, or
2. initiate a rolling maul.

The role of the other support players at a maul is simply to try to maintain or generate forward momentum and provide solid, wide protection for the ball. They must drive in on either side of the original ball-carrier and concentrate on keeping him and the opposition on their feet. They must try to keep their inside legs back to provide targets for subsequent support players to hit. Upper bodies should be parallel to the ground with spines in line with the direction of play. At least two support players should have their heads where they can see the ball.

Start a rolling maul

The rolling maul

If your opponents manage to stop you going forwards and have defenders standing off at the sides of the maul, the best tactic is to start a rolling maul. This may help you to regenerate forward momentum and will commit the fringe defenders to active defence.

To start a rolling maul, you must have solid control, with the ball at or near the back. Feel for any point of weakness in the opposition resistance. The last support player should drive to widen the maul on that side. The ball-carrier should then push the ball into that player, who in turn should secure it with one hand and arm and with his other arm pull the passer to him. By swinging his back into the fringe defenders, he can swing the original ball-carrier around the outside of the maul. The last support player on the other side of the maul can now come across and drive in on the ball-carrier to continue the rolling action. Unless a rolling maul sets a ball-carrier completely free and running forwards into space, the ball should be released to your scrum-half once the maul has gone beyond your opponents' first line of defence and is moving forwards.

Defending against rucks and mauls

The basic principle is to stop your opponents going forwards and only to commit enough players to achieve this. The easiest way to stop them is to put the ball-carrier on the ground or

to wheel a ruck using only a few players. In a maul your front-line defenders should try to get their hands on the ball. All players not involved in stopping the opposition should concentrate on defence close to the sides of the ruck or maul.

Back play

Importance and objectives

If you play in the backs you must be a complete rugby player. You must be able to run quickly, strongly and elusively; catch, pass and kick the ball; tackle and resist tackles and even ruck and maul when required. Above all, you must think quickly and be able to make split-second judgements. Concentrate on performing these basic skills consistently well, and you will never let your team down.

Every member of a back division has specific positional responsibilities, but it is also important for backs to work together. This may be as a full unit or in smaller groups or pairs. Nine times out of ten it is team-work that produces the best results, rather than purely individual brilliance. This is not to say that individual flair is not important. On the contrary, it is the unexpected action of individual players that often transforms an unpromising situation into a piece of exciting, positive rugby. However, it is generally the preceding actions of other players

Nos 14 and 15 provide effective support for the scrum-half

that create the opportuntities for individuals to sparkle. Team-work and a common sense of purpose are therefore essential. If one person fails in his allotted task, the whole team is put under pressure.

Backs must constantly be aware of the major principles of play: go forwards, ball-carrier in front, continuity, support, control, pressure and decision making. In support of these principles, the main objectives of back play are:

1. to initiate and develop attacks
2. to support and develop attacks started by the forwards
3. to play a major role in team defence.

In pursuit of these objectives there are two important concepts to understand.

The gain line

This is an imaginary line drawn across the field parallel to the goal-lines through the point where your team wins possession. Until you move the ball forwards beyond that line, you will not have gained any ground. Invariably, because of the laws and the nature of the game, the first movement of the ball is back from the source of possession towards your own line. Backs must be aware that their primary objective is to advance the ball beyond the gain line, preferably by getting a ball-carrier ahead of the rest of the team and ultimately over their opponents' goal-line.

You must get beyond the gain line

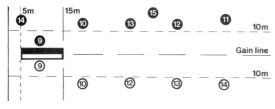

The gain line

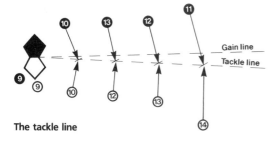

The tackle line

The tackle line

It would be easy to carry the ball beyond the gain line if there was nothing to stop you, but there are of course defenders. The tackle line is an imaginary line across the field, mid-way between the attackers and defenders at the moment the attacking team wins the ball. If they run towards each other at the same speed, it is the point where contact will be made. The position of the tackle line varies depending on the respective starting positions of the attack

and defence. The attackers will naturally try to ensure that the point of contact occurs beyond the gain line, whereas the defenders will be trying to make their tackles before the attackers reach the gain line.

It is essential that in any situation not only the backs, but the whole team, are aware of the relative positions of the gain and tackle lines.

Key factors

There are four key factors in effective back play: possession, position, pace and purpose.

Possession

Possession is usually hard-earned, and will often be the result of long periods of intense physical effort by the main ball winners, your forwards. As a back, therefore, your first duty is to make the best possible use of any possession provided. You must also try to ensure that your team keeps the ball for as long as possible, ideally until a try is scored. Treat possession like gold, and never waste hard-earned ball by indiscriminate kicking or sloppy handling.

If you are held by an opponent, try to stay on your feet, and fight to protect the ball and keep it available for your support players. Don't make optimistic passes out of contact situations.

**Don't kick away
hard-earned possession**

Remember, you are responsible for the ball until you have scored a try or have delivered the ball safely into the hands of a team-mate. If you are properly tackled and have to release the ball, make sure you fall with your body between the ball and your opponent and release the ball back towards your support players.

There are times when you must also act as a ball winner, especially following tackles in mid-field. Don't just rush off to position yourself for the next attack, leaving the ball to be won by the forwards. If you are the nearest support player to a tackle, go in and get your hands on the ball if possible, or at least drive in to provide a platform on which later support can build. Backs must be able to ruck and maul as well as forwards can.

Position

You must be aware of the importance of position. Positional awareness relates to each individual, the units, the whole team and the opposition. At any given moment in any situation, you should ask yourself four questions.

1. Where am I on the field?
2. Where is the ball, where is it likely to come from and where is it likely to go to?
3. Where are the opposition?
4. Where are the rest of my team?

The answers to these four basic questions should largely determine your subsequent actions. They should also lead you to secondary questions, the answers to which should help you to make correct decisions. Possible questions include the following.

1. Am I in the right position to receive the ball and the best position to make good use of it?
2. Where will the defenders go once they are on the move and we are moving?
3. Where will my support come from?

Such advance judgement should not be followed blindly, but should form the basis for immediate action at the critical moment of decision. What often looks like an instantaneous reaction on the field is usually the product of advance information and previous experience. However, the movements of players and the ball are never wholly predictable and must not be assumed to be so.

Positional awareness comes largely from experience but it can be developed by intelligent self-questioning.

Pace

Superior speed is often the only mark of distinction between one player and another, and the higher the level at which you play, the more

You must know where the space is and where your support is

Which way will the attacker go next?

important pace becomes. Whatever team you play for, the skills involved are basically the same, but international rugby is faster than county rugby; county rugby is faster than senior club 1st-XV level; senior club is faster than junior club; and 1st XV is faster than 2nd XV.

Your running speed can be improved by working at your personal fitness. The speed at which you can move the ball can be greatly improved by regular practice of your skills under pressure. Your speed of thought can be developed through experience, by practising against opposition and by thoughtful self-questioning and analysis.

But remember, pace must be controlled, and must be related to the fourth key factor, purpose.

Purpose

Everything you do on the field should have a positive purpose: positive in that you should set out to make things happen rather than letting events take their course and merely reacting to situations as they develop; purposeful in that every action should be preceded by a question process of 'where? what? why? when? how? who?'.

For example, imagine you are at full-back and your opponents kick the ball high towards you. You must quickly decide what to do and your thoughts should run as follows. Where

am I on the field: inside or outside the 22m line; in the centre; or towards the left or right touch-line? Where are my opponents: very close or well away; coming from in front or from the left or right? Where are my nearest support players?

What could I possibly do after I catch the ball: kick to touch; kick ahead and follow up; kick across into space; start a counter-attack by running and taking on opponents or by linking with support players; run into touch; run behind my own line and concede a five-metre scrum; take a tackle and hope to win the ensuing ruck or maul?

Why should I do any of these things? How am I going to do it? Which techniques are appropriate in this situation? Who is going to be involved other than myself? Are they capable of supporting me in the way I require, e.g. is a prop capable of continuing the counter-attack or is the winger capable of supporting in a ruck or maul?

Obviously, there are many, many variables and equally obviously such thoughts will have to be compressed into fractions of seconds even though some aspects of decision making can be based upon previous experience. But don't just do things out of habit, remember your aim is to act with a positive purpose. Why and when are nearly always more important than how. Possession, position, pace and purpose are important factors for the whole team. They are essential for good back play.

Back play – individual responsibilities

The back division consists of seven players: scrum-half, the link between forwards and backs; fly-half and two centres, the mid-field or front three; the two wings and full-back, the back three.

These players must be able to work together effectively in their sub-groups and as a full unit, but they also have individual responsibilities. Some of these are common to all backs. You must never miss a tackle; you must never drop a pass or give a poor pass to a team-mate; you must never give a pass to someone in a worse position than yourself; you must be prepared to take on and try to run past your opposite number; and you must be aware of the principles of play and the key factors for effective back play.

Other responsibilities, skills and techniques are specific to the position you play.

Scrum-half

The scrum-half is the crucial link between the forwards and backs. You are in an ideal position to control the play of your team by guiding and directing the efforts of your forwards and by making the first key decision once the ball is released by them.

Because you occupy such a critical position, you must have a complete range of skills at your disposal. Particularly, you must be able to pass the ball quickly off either hand and kick effectively with either foot. As you will put the ball into the scrum and normally receive it facing the right touch-line, your left hand is your more important passing hand and your right foot your more important kicking foot.

Allied to these skills you must have the basic qualities of speed, strength and stamina, together with agility, resilience, alertness, awareness, adaptability, confidence, composure and courage.

Speed of thought and action is essential in a position in which you will invariably be under pressure, as you will rarely escape the attentions of defenders at scrum, line-out, ruck and maul, courage and resilience are indispensable. Above all, you must remain calm under pressure and display an air of confidence, which must be transmitted to the pack in front of you and to the backs outside you.

There are several specific techniques you must master.

Spin pass

This is the bread-and-butter pass of the modern scrum-half. It should be used whenever you have sufficient time and reasonable length is required. This type of pass combines speed, length and accuracy, and allows you to remain on your feet so that you can support quickly after passing. Unless you are very quick and skilful, however, it is a vulnerable pass when you are under great pressure.

Assuming you are passing to the left and the ball is on the ground, the key factors of the technique are as follows.

1. Body and feet positions: Move to the ball in a low, crouched position, with knees bent and eyes on the ball. Get your right foot close to and just to the right of the ball. Your weight at this moment should be on your right foot.
2. Weight shift: Keep your hands to the right of your body and, as you reach for the ball, stretch your left leg towards your target. Keep this leg out of the line of your pass so that your arms can sweep through freely. A wide base is necessary for power and length.
3. Grasp and sweep: Your hands and arm should come into the ball from the right and in one movement grasp the ball with fingers

Spin pass to the left

Spin pass to the right

spread on either side and sweep it away towards your target. Drive strongly off your right leg and, as your arms begin to extend, press with your right hand and roll your wrist over the ball as you release it. This action imparts spin, which gives the ball a stable flight. The hand further from the target is always the dominant hand.

Speed is important, and you must resist the temptation to pick the ball up and then swing your arms back to start the pass. It must be

swept off the ground. If you are not threatened by an opponent you can increase the length of your arm swing and the length of your pass by initially placing your right foot to the left of the ball. Speed is generally more important than length, however.

If the ball is passed to you from a line-out or a maul, the key factors are to establish a broad base and use the weight shift to start your pass.

On every pass, keep your upper body and head down and make sure that the shoulder of your control arm drives right through on the line

Pivot pass

of your pass. Aim for a fairly high trajectory. Your fly-half should receive the ball at about shoulder height.

If you cannot spin pass equally well off either hand you can get yourself into position to use your stronger hand by pivoting. To do this the technique is much the same but you need a little more time. In addition, although you receive the ball facing forwards, you actually pass with your back to your opponents. Passing to the left off your right hand, push up off your right leg as you receive the ball and pull your left shoulder back and round towards your target. Keep the ball back towards your right hip. As you come round, stretch your left leg towards your target, drop into a crouch and pass as before. If you are right-hand dominant, this pass can be particularly useful from line-outs on the left-hand side of the field.

Dive pass

If you are under extreme pressure or if you have to go back to a ball rolling away from you, the dive pass is the most effective technique to use.

The key factors are as follows:

1. Body and feet positions: Approach from directly behind the ball, ideally along the intended line of your pass. Crouch low and put your right foot just behind and to the right of the ball. Your left foot should be about 30cm behind to give you a narrow base.
2. Weight shift: Grasp the ball with both hands, fingers spread on either side. Drive from your legs, keeping your shoulders going beyond the ball towards your target. Keep the ball back and down towards your waist.
3. Pull and thrust: As your body extends, look up at your target. This will bring your strong back muscles into play and add power. At full stretch, pull the ball up with bent elbows and thrust it towards your target, extending your arms and fingers right through on the line of the pass.

The pivot dive pass is started in much the same way as a pivot spin pass. The main difference is that the standing pass is made off a wide base whereas the dive pass starts from a narrow base.

To achieve consistently good results, the most important things to concentrate on are getting your body and feet quickly into the correct position to make the pass. Too many scrum-halves concentrate on getting their hands on the ball as their first priority.

Dive pass

A pivot dive under pressure

Putting the ball into a scrum

It is most important for a scrum-half to be able to put the ball into a scrum well and in a consistent manner. Your skill in doing this has a definite influence on whether or not your hooker wins the ball.

The manner in which the ball is put in is tightly controlled by the laws. You must put the ball in without delay, as soon as the two front rows have closed together, and on the side first chosen, which should always be the left side. You must stand one metre from the scrum mid-way between the two front rows. The ball must be held with both hands mid-way between your ankle and knee, and from that position you must put the ball into the scrum with a single forward movement (no backswing or dummying is allowed). The ball must be put in at a quick speed straight along the middle line so that it first touches the ground immediately beyond the width of the nearest prop's shoulders.

It can be helpful to stand with your legs together to avoid the possibility of a backswing. To give your hooker some assistance, hold the ball near the points with the end in your right hand angled slightly towards your hooker. This presents the broad side of the ball for him to strike. Timing your put-in with his strike is the most important thing to practise. Ideally he should be able to react to the movement of your hands, but if he finds that difficult, your hooker should control the timing by tapping with the fingers or hand of his nearest arm.

It is essential that you are methodical and consistent in your preparations and delivery, and you must be prepared to adapt your technique to suit the requirements of the referee when necessary.

Pivot kick

The pivot kick is another essential weapon in a scrum-half's armoury, It is mainly required when you are kicking to touch under pressure from scrums and line-outs in your own 22m and for high kicks ahead from set pieces outside your 22m. If differs from the normal high kick in that you will usually be facing the touch-line or even your goal-line when kicking, and as you will probably be under pressure and need instant height, your point of contact with the ball will be much higher than 45 degrees to the ground.

If you are kicking with your right foot, the key factors are as follows.

1. Keep your weight directly over your left leg.
2. Keep the ball fairly close to your body and place it across your kicking foot so that you strike the broadest part of the ball.
3. Keep your right knee high and your foot flexed but tensed to hook the ball in the required direction.
4. Make the point of contact up towards waist height.
5. Drive off your bent left leg as you kick.
6. Keep your body turned away from oncoming opponents to shield the ball and avoid a charge-down.

Kicking from a scrum near touch

Rolling diagonal kick

The rolling diagonal kick is needed at scrum-half to keep your pack going forwards outside your 22m, especially from scrums and static mauls in the centre and to the right side of the field. The technique is essentially that of the grub kick.

The scrum-half in attack

Passing

Your first duty is to provide your fly-half with a consistent, accurate service, putting the ball where he wants it when he wants it. Basically your fly-half will want the ball in front of him at about shoulder height, but sometimes he will be standing still, sometimes running quickly at a right angle across the line of your pass, and sometimes he will drift away along the line of your pass. At times he will stand deep but on other occasions he will require a flat pass. Mastery of all your passing techniques and regular practice with your partner are the only ways to achieve consistency.

However, your team will suffer if you merely pass every ball you receive to your fly-half. There are times when you must accept responsibility for varying play by kicking or running, particularly if your backs are under pressure or are not being successful in beating the defence.

Kicking

Your two main attacking kicks are the high kick and the rolling diagonal kick.

You will probably need to use a high kick when you receive a slow or untidy ball from a line-out – particularly when it has been deflected and gathered in – or from a scrum on the right-hand 15m line, or from a static ruck or maul on the right side of the field.

You must get your team going forwards, so hoist a high kick parallel to the touch-line, ideally along the 5m line. Remember, you do not want to give a free catch and clearance kick to your opponents, so your kick has to give your team a chance of regaining possession. A good player will run 25 to 30 metres in between four and five seconds, therefore if you want your support players to arrive under your kick, the ball must stay in the air for at least $4\frac{1}{2}$ seconds and not land more than 25 metres from where you kick.

Use the rolling kick when you receive the ball slowly from scrums or from static rucks and mauls where the opposition are lined up on the offside line to pressurise your backs. Your first move should often be towards your opponents, looking for a gap through which to tread the ball. Ideally your kick should be deep enough to make their mid-field players turn towards their own line but shallow enough to bring their

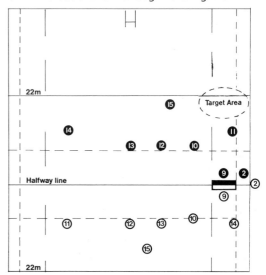

Scrum-half kicking from a line-out

full-back forwards and give your own players a chance to reach the ball first.

Remember, every time you kick you are temporarily giving away hard-earned possession, so never kick the ball straight to your opponents so that they can use it. The objectives are to get your team going forwards and to regain possession as quickly as possible. If your support players cannot gather the kick they should at least aim to drive the receiver backwards so that your team gets the put-in at a subsequent scrummage.

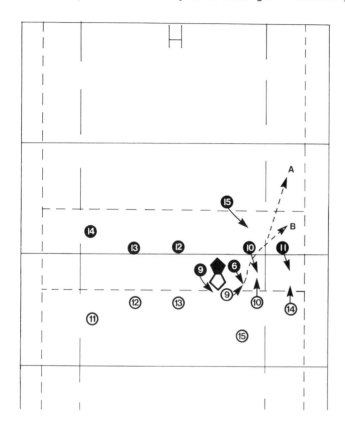

Scrum-half kicking from a scrum on the right of the field. *A* **Long rolling kick to turn the Black (15).** *B* **Short rolling kick just behind Black (11)**

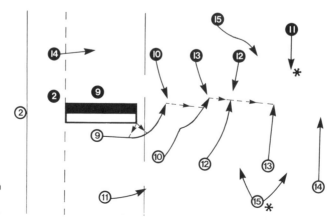

Scrum-half attacking run from a line-out. Note options open to players

Kicking from a mid-field scrum

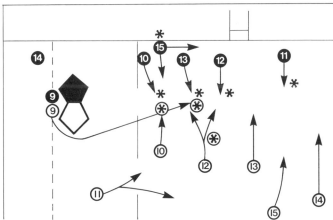

Scrum-half attacking run from a scrum. Note the points of decision-making this creates and all options open to players

Running

Apart from providing your fly-half with a steady stream of good passes, the most important contribution you can make to your team's efforts in attack is to pose a constant threat to the opposition defence. If you can make them aware of the need to defend close to the source of possession, and cause uncertainty in their defensive organisation, it will relieve pressure on your mid-field players. Your most effective way of doing this is to run with the ball.

Knowing when to run and when to pass will only come with experience, but you must be prepared to run when the right opportunity presents itself. Line-outs present the fewest opportunities, but occasionally a flat run taking a deflection from the tail of the line can be effective. You are quickly among the mid-field

defence if you get past the end player and could create an extra-player situation.

At scrums the defence is usually well organised but breaks are possible given certain conditions. Three examples are given below.

1. Scrum five metres from the opponents' line, 15m in from the right touch-line. Your pack win the ball, control it at No. 8 and drive forwards. Defending flankers and No. 8 must stay down to prevent a push-over try, and there is a great chance for you to score between the scrum and the right touch-line.
2. At scrums where the defending flankers are breaking off early and drifting wide to pressurise your mid-field, there is a chance to get through behind them.
3. From scrums on the left of the field near your opponents' line, a fast, flat run to the right can create many scoring possibilities.

Rucks and mauls often provide the best opportunities for impromptu running by the scrum-half. Often the defence has only one player at each side and occasionally none if they are all committed. Look for such situations, and if the ball comes quickly be prepared to go for a possible break in the same direction as the original movement of the attack. This will fully stretch the cover defence and reduce the possibility of running into stragglers arriving late to the breakdown.

Whenever you run, however, be clear *why* you are running instead of passing or kicking, and think about what happens *next*.

The scrum-half in defence

You have two main roles in defence:

1. when you receive the ball very near your own line
2. as a defender when your opponents have the ball.

When you receive the ball in defensive situations you must be prepared to take the responsibility for clearing to touch, especially from good ball from mauls and line-outs. From scrums it is generally better to move the ball to your fly-half or full-back, as you will be under pressure unless you are near the right touch-line or your pack is really rolling forwards.

If you receive bad ball in defence, never compound the fault by passing it further back towards your own line. Even if you can't gain ground, get the ball safely into touch. At least your team then has another chance to win the ball and you can organise your defence. Good ball won unexpectedly from line-outs in defence on the opposition throw can often be used to turn defence into attack. Get the ball quickly to your fly-half. He must then make the next decision.

As a defender when your opponents have the ball, you have three specific situations to be concerned with: scrums, rucks and mauls, and line-outs.

Scrums are the most important of these. Your task is to be responsible for your immediate opponent or the first attacker on the put-in side. Try to pressurise your opponent at all times. Stay close to him as he puts the ball in and follow the ball through the scrum. If possible, grab his nearer arm as he gets the ball, but take care to keep your feet behind the ball; it is better to let your opponents have it than to concede a penalty.

It is not always good policy to follow your opponent around the scrum. If his pack are channelling well and rolling forwards, it might be preferable to wait behind your pack so that you can cover an attack on the left side of your scrum. If you follow round in such situations, you will always be on the wrong side of play, not between the ball and your goal-line. Near your own line you may need to be responsible for the opposing fly-half or first centre, depending on your team's defensive organisation, but you must first ensure that your immediate opponent, their scrum-half, does not try to sneak past you.

At rucks and mauls, when it seems likely that your opponents will win the ball, take up a position just behind the back foot of your players and about one metre to the side. Generally you should choose the side away from the direction of the original attack, i.e. the far side if your were running across to get there. This is the side more likely to be attacked by your opponents and allows one of your covering forwards, usually the last to arrive, to be responsible for the near side.

From line-outs your chief role is in cover defence, always aiming to keep between the ball and your goal-line and as near to the ball as possible.

The scrum-half controller

As you are the link between forwards and backs you must take responsibility for guiding and directing the work of your forwards. You are in an ideal postion to help them as you should be able to see what is happening to the ball, your players and your opponents. Crisp, confident directions are essential and, if necessary, a code of signals should be devised and agreed in practice.

At scrums on your ball you must ensure that your forwards know what is expected of them, that they know where the ball is going initially and, if appropriate, what the backs are likely to do. Similarly, your backs must know if a back-row attack is planned. You must have good communication with your No. 8 to ensure you receive the ball when and where you want it. He must know whether to release the ball to his right, to pick up and feed you or to pick up and drive.

At line-outs you are ideally placed to relay the signals to jumpers and the thrower, and at rucks and mauls you should direct the efforts of the players involved. Tell them where the ball is; point out which arms and legs need to be moved; tell them when to roll off and drive, hold the ball, or release it quickly. You are a key decision maker in these situations. Do not shirk your responsibilities.

Fly-half

Fly-half is a key position in a team. You must be a complete player, with mastery of all the individual skills of handling, running, kicking and contact. In addition to the physical skills you need good awareness, the ability to assess situations and make quick decisions, positional sense, and an enterprising, imaginative and positive attitude. You should be the mid-field general, the tactical director of your team's play,

and as such must recognise and be prepared to accept this responsibility.

Handling

You must be able to catch everything your scrum-half throws at you and be able to transfer the ball to your centres, in one stride if necessary. You must be able to make long 'miss' passes, loop passes and switch passes to the left and right with equal dexterity. These techniques are described in the section on individual handling but, above all, you must know when to make these passes and why you are using them.

Running

Control of pace is perhaps your most important requirement and you must recognise the effect your running speed has (before and after you receive the ball) on your own players and on your opponents.

A side-step and swerve are valuable assets. You will often find a side-step more useful in defensive situations than in attack, particularly

Fly-half is a key position

when you are under pressure and have to create space for yourself to make a clearing kick or to launch a counter-attack. In attack you will rarely be in a good position to side-step from set pieces, as you would probably run into defenders, but in broken play it can be devastating.

A swerve is probably the more important weapon in your armoury. It enables you to change your line of running relatively smoothly and, while forcing your opponents to adjust their positions, it is easier for your support runners (centres particularly) to follow than a side-step. You will find that a good swerve is necessary to make an effective switch pass and for running off a loop pass. If the opposing centres come up too fast in defence at a scrum, it is a swerve that is more effective in taking you outside your opposite number and into the space behind them. The techniques of swerve and side-step are described in the section on individual running.

Kicking

To be really effective at fly-half you must be able to kick well with either foot. If you are right-footed only and receive the ball from scrum or line-out on the right of the field, you will not be able to kick down that side unless you stop and turn in that direction. This is a common failing, but it does make it very easy for your opponents to predict what you are going to do with the ball, so work to develop equal ability with both feet.

You will be largely responsible for the tactical kicking of your team and, despite the pleas to curb the amount of kicking in a match, it must be recognised that kicking is an integral feature of the game. Remember, however, that whenever you kick the ball you are temporarily giving away hard-earned possession, so you must always know why you are kicking and be specific in your objectives. Never kick the ball instinctively or just because you cannot think of anything else to do.

Most of your tactical attacking kicking should be from scrums, or from slow rucks/mauls, particularly those between your own 22m line and your opponents' 10m line. In your own

22m area you will normally kick for touch. Never kick inside your opponents' 22m zone and only occasionally between their 22m and 10m lines.

From line-outs your inside centre should do most of the kicking. When you receive good ball from line-outs the opposition backs will be 10 to 20 metres away and if you kick immediately they will have less distance to run to the ball than your centres and wings. If you hold the ball to bring them towards you, you are likely to be under pressure from their last players in the line-out, so move it to your inside centre. This will bring their backs up, including their open-side wing, and create more space behind them. Your centre should make the decision whether to kick into this space, move the ball on, or attack by running.

The main kicks you will need at scrums are the high kick ahead, the long diagonal kick, and the short, angled grub kick.

The high kick ahead and the long diagonal kick are mainly for gaining ground and producing a position on the field from which you can regain possession and create a score. With high kicks, you must give your support

The high kick ahead

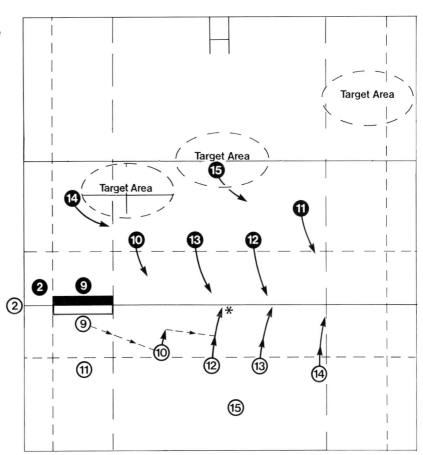

Tactical kicking from a line-out. Note the possible target areas

players a chance to regain the ball. Use the formula described in the scrum-half section, i.e. kick approximately 25 metres with the ball in the air for $4\frac{1}{2}$ seconds at least. Your target area will depend upon the position from which you kick but your usual options will be:

1. between the 5m and 15m line just outside your opponents' 22m line
2. in front of the posts just outside their 22m line
3. either of these positions inside their 22m area.

Your aim is for your support players to get their hands to the ball as it comes down or at least to catch your opponents in possession or force them to clear hurriedly, probably to touch. This gives you the advantage of the throw at the subsequent line-out.

You should use the long diagonal kick only sparingly, aiming for the space behind their open-side winger. Unless you have got good communication with your own winger on that side, he will find it very difficult to put pressure on the opposition, so if you use this kick it must be very accurately weighted and placed.

On no account should you kick so that the opposing full-back or wings can catch the ball on the run and initiate a counter-attack. Kick very high to pin them under the ball, or long so that they have to turn to collect it. You should know which is the defender's weaker foot and place your kick so that he has to use that foot.

The shorter diagonal kick from scrums or slow rucks/mauls on either side of the field is a useful weapon in your armoury. This kick should be aimed into the space behind their winger and weighted so that it stops on or about the 5m line. If your support runners cannot get to

Short diagonal kick

the ball first, your minimum objective is to force the defence to put the ball into touch under pressure so that your team gets a line-out throw-in at a good, attacking position.

The grub kick should not be pre-planned, but should be a reserve alternative if an attempted break is obviously due to fail. On many occasions, players kick through a gap they could run through. The grub kick is most effective if the opposing centres are coming up quickly in defence. In this case, take a flat pass from your scrum-half and run at your opposite number. Swerve out and aim for the gap between him and his inside centre. If it is obvious that he is going to tackle you, look to see if you can get a pass behind his centre to your players coming through. If not, now is the time to drop the ball onto your outside foot and push it through the gap. Your kick should be deep enough to make their open-side wing turn back but not so that their full-back has time to gather and clear easily.

Re-start kicks from the 22m and half-way lines are usually the responsibility of the fly-half, so even if you are not the team goal-kicker, you should be able to place kick and drop kick accurately. It is so important to give your team a chance to regain possession at re-starts that you must be able to hit the target area for these kicks consistently. Depending on your team's preference, from half-way this is usually just beyond the 10m line, landing on the 5m line.

As an option the landing point can be the 15m line but it is more difficult to get sufficient height over this shorter distance. At 22m re-starts the target should be a 5m square beyond the 22m line and in from touch. At fly-half, you are also often in a position to score by using a drop kick for goal, so you must practise these skills.

Fakes, feints and dummies

Allied to your handling, running and kicking skills, it is to your advantage if you can successfully conceal your intentions from your opponents in any given situation. Cultivate the art of deception. The use of fakes, feints and dummies can gain valuable split seconds and an extra metre of space for you and your team-mates in attack and defence. Sudden changes of pace and direction, false starts and stops, shaping to kick then passing or running, and other similar movements can cause momentary hesitation by defenders and help you to carry out your true intentions with a little less pressure.

Awareness and decision making

Your most important function at fly-half is that of controller and coordinator. Key decisions concerning the way you use the ball have to be made, and this effectively makes you the tactical director of your team. This responsibility also applies to defence, where you must try to ensure that the rest of the backs are in the right place at the right time.

Your ability to make accurate judgements is vital, and to make correct decisions you need information. This can only be gained by a process of thoughtful observation and rapid analysis: what is usually known as 'reading the game'.

Try to develop a method of analysing situations that through practice and experience will become automatic and will help you to react very quickly whenever necessary.

Obviously you never have time in a match to go through all the possible combinations of questions this method offers but, used selectively, it will provide the information you need to add to that already stored in your mind.

Decision making in advance is easy, but it is your ability to make decisions at critical moments that is really important. At fly-half you can never afford to stop thinking.

Positional play

There are four elements to your positional play at fly-half: depth, width, line of running and speed of running. You must appreciate the ways in which these factors influence your actions and also how they affect your support players and the defence. Different combinations produce a variety of effects and you must always decide what you are trying to do and position yourself accordingly.

Depth
Depth is your position relative to the gain line. It will vary if you are in attack or defence, depending on the source of possession and on the positions of defenders. Depth gives you space and time, but it also gives your opponents space and time. You must decide how much depth you need in any particular situation and weigh that against how much it is desirable to allow the opposition.

Generally speaking, if you are going for a break you should take the ball flat and try to penetrate quickly. If you are moving the ball

Where you stand is important

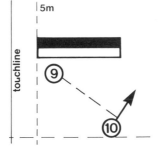

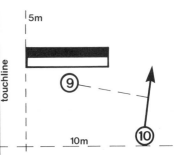

Fly-half positioning affects running angles

wide you need just enough space to allow you to get the ball to where it is intended.

If you are kicking you need just enough time to make your kick safely. Too flat and you risk a charge-down, too deep and you have further to run to the ball than the defenders do. At line-outs you never need more than ten metres back from the line of touch. In defence, you should always be on the offside line (when the opposition have the ball).

Width
Width relates to the distance you stand from your scrum-half on a line across the field. It will largely be determined by the length of your scrum-half's pass and the position of defenders.

In general, you should stand as wide as possible in attack – and remember, your width tends to dictate your line of running. Occasionally from line-outs you may decide to stand closer than necessary to bring the opposing flanker at you on a straight line. This makes it easier for you to beat him on the outside and makes drift defence more difficult for the opposition; it also enables you to give a pop pass to your inside centre for him to carry the ball forwards beyond the gain line.

In defence, you will normally be aiming to be just inside your opposite number.

Line of running
Depth and width really refer to static positions, but the most important aspect of positional play is positioning on the run.

Basically you should try to run as straight as possible in attack and not push your centres across the field. However, you will have to

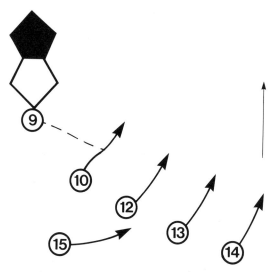

Centres are being pushed across due to poor alignment of the fly-half

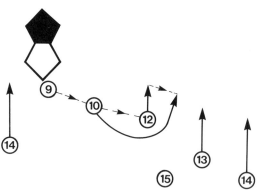

By altering the positional depth, more options are created

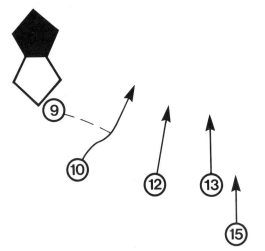

By standing wider, no. 12 can now run straighter and allow 13, 14 and 15 to run straight

adjust to the speed and height of your scrum-half's pass and this, together with your original position, will largely determine your line of running. In defence you will be aiming for the inside hip of your opponent, so his movements will determine your line.

Speed of running

You should not always run onto the pass at the same speed. Indeed, it is not even necessary to run onto the ball at all in some situations. It must depend on what you are trying to do. If you run towards your opponents, you are cutting down not only your time and space but also that of the players outside you. The faster you run, the quicker you reduce this time and space. There is little point in standing deep if you are going to close the gap either before or after you get the ball. If you do not want a gap, take the ball flat at pace. If you do require space, take the ball slowly or even standing still.

Remember also that your running speed influences that of the players outside you. If you want them to add pace to the attack, don't go too quickly initially.

The fly-half in attack

Although your main role in attack may well be that of controller and coordinator, you must not neglect your individual responsibility for taking on the opposition. If you never pose a threat to the defence, there is little reason for them to mark you and this enables them to put added pressure on the players outside you. Your ability to threaten them will depend on the evasive running skills you possess and on your ability to vary your play skilfully. You should never be predictable; the defence must never be sure whether you are going to run, pass or kick. On the other hand you must not confuse your own players, otherwise you will find yourself without support.

Try to achieve a balance in your attacking play. Your first duty is to enable your team to achieve its objectives and, although you always have an important role to play in attack, it does not have to be a starring role.

The importance of tactical kicking has already been described. On most other occasions when you receive the ball in attack, you should be trying to create opportunities for your team-mates to play their part effectively. This usually means making the initial decision about what to do, then moving the ball on at the right time.

Only occasionally should you look for or try to force a break. The opportunities to break usually occur naturally and are most likely in broken play and from rucks and mauls. On these occasions defenders are quite likely to be caught out of position and you must be ready to exploit any gaps.

At scrums the opposing backs are usually closing rapidly, committed to a line of running and course of action. Momentary hesitation, uncertainty or error of judgement on their part can again present opportunities for you to exploit. The further you are away from them, however, the more time they have to redeem themselves before you get there.

If you take the ball deep you have little chance of making a break, and so at line-outs you should not expect any chances at all.

The other role in attack that you must not neglect is that of support runner. Too many fly-halves pass the ball, then relax and watch the ensuing proceedings from a distance. 'Pass and follow' should be your catch-phrase. If you move the ball early you are unlikely to be tackled as you pass and will therefore be free to support. When the ball is moved to the wing you should always be the first or second support runner, ready to take a pass inside or outside.

The fly-half in defence

The fly-half has a specific job to do in defence only when the opposition win the ball at scrums and line-outs.

At scrums you are responsible for marking your opposite number, but the way you do this will depend upon your team tactics. Normally, you will have the assistance of the flanker on your side of the scrum. If you want to stop your opponent linking with his centres, stand and run slightly outside him, forcing him in towards your flanker. Don't go too wide, however, or their fly-half will go behind you and link with his centres. If you want to drive him away from his forwards, go up on his inside hip. On no account must you allow him to run past your outside shoulder and, if he is receiving the ball slowly, try to put as much pressure on him as possible. This could cause him to stand deeper at subsequent scrums, which will limit his attacking options still further.

If your opponent passes the ball on while you are some distance from him, quickly alter your

The fly-half is an important defender

If your opponent moves the ball early, move out one place, or provide cover in depth. Good communication with your centres is vital and remember, when the opposition have the ball, your work in defence is never done until your team have regained possession.

Centre threequarter

Playing in the centre is the most demanding position in the back division and one of the most difficult positions in the team. This is mainly because the contribution you can make to your team's efforts is largely dependent upon the ability and actions of your forwards and half-backs.

At centre you must have all the skills of a fly-half with particular emphasis on swift, sure handling and strong tackling. You must be prepared to do a lot of unrewarded running, both in attack and defence. You must be able to make swift decisions in reaction to situations that occur unexpectedly, and you must remain cool, calm and composed under pressure.

The particular handling skills you require are the one-pace, 'miss', loop, switch and screen passes. Your evasive running skills must include swerve, side-step and change of pace, together with a range of fakes, feints and dummies.

Kicking should not be a prominent feature of your play but you should be competent with both feet and be able to screw kick to touch from defence, make long diagonal kicks from line-outs, and execute occasional short grub kicks in mid-field.

line of running towards their inside centre. Both your centres may also be able to move across one place but, if they are already committed, you should cover across immediately behind them. Your inside centre should always know where you are and you should normally be just ahead of him when going forwards to make tackles from scrums.

At line-outs, the last player in your line of forwards is ten metres nearer their fly-half than you are. He should be primarily responsible for making the first tackle. This leaves you free to go for their inside centre with your centres moving out one place. However, you must be ready to tackle your immediate opponent if your tail-end forward gets caught up in the line-out. This is particularly likely if the ball is thrown long at the line-out.

Centre is a demanding position

The centre threequarter, with his concentration fixed firmly on the ball, displays good handling skills

You must have a full range of contact skills, particularly the ability to make and take hard tackles at speed. In contact situations your ability to win or protect the ball is crucial and you must be as good as the flankers at rucking and mauling. You do not have to be big and strong but it certainly helps. Pace is your most valuable attacking weapon, however, and you must constantly strive to improve your sprinting ability, particularly acceleration over short distances.

The centre in attack

Playing in the centre you have basically three functions to perform:

1. integral member of the back division
2. individual attacker
3. support player.

Which particular role you play in any situation will depend upon the objectives and development of the attack, the position and actions of defenders and, if you receive the ball, what has happened up to that point. You must be flexible in your attitude and capable of rapidly assessing what is required of you at any specific moment. In particular you must be positive, for in the centre it is absolutely true to say that 'he who hesitates is lost'. The best centres are those who make the right decisions quickest and most often.

Positional play

Assuming your handling and running skills are sound, the next most important feature of your play is your positioning. Like the fly-half, you must be conscious of depth, width, lines of running and speed of running.

Depth

Depth at centre is simply a matter of ensuring that you are always in the correct position to receive a pass from the nearest player with the ball. This will usually be your fly-half or co-centre. They will want to pass the ball sideways and in front of you, and as a rule of thumb you should position yourself so that you can just see the number on the passer's shirt (or the place where it would be). The wider you stand, the deeper you must stand, and remember also that your starting position is not as important as being in the right position on the move.

There will be times when you need to stand in a flat position, when you are taking a loop pass or when you know that the team-mate inside you is going to kick, but for most of the time you must try to maintain your depth from the ball.

Width

How wide you are in relation to the players inside you should vary according to what you are trying to do. Sometimes you will want to take a short pass at speed to punch past your opponent's inside arm. At other times you may take a long pass to try to get outside a defender.

When you are at inside centre, however, it is important that you stand well away from your fly-half. Wherever he stands he will have to adjust to the speed and length of his scrum-half's pass. Usually this means he will drift out and across the field as he takes the ball. If you start deep and close to him you will find yourself being pushed across however well you try to maintain your position, and the players outside you will suffer accordingly. If you stand wide you can hold your line of running, and as the fly-half drifts out you will be in a good position to take his pass.

81

Try to run straight

Lines of running

The importance of lines of running in the centre cannot be over-estimated. You must try to run almost parallel to the touch-line unless a specific move calls for a variation. Your starting position largely determines the line you run on, so remember depth and width. Turning your shoulders towards the ball and standing with your outside leg forwards will at least help you to set off in the right direction.

The advantages of straight running over diagonal running are as follows.

1. It is easier to side-step and swerve.
2. It is easier to pass to either side.
3. It is difficult for your opponent to align himself on your inside hip.
4. Because it increases your options, it can cause a defender to be flat-footed. Once he is checked he can be beaten by change of pace.
5. Players outside you can run on straight lines and are not crowded out towards the touch-line.
6. It is the shortest route to the gain line and to your opponents' goal-line.
7. You can see clearly on either side as you run.
8. Support running is easier from all positions.

There are no real disadvantages to running on straight lines (unless you are a coward), but it is incredible how many players still run sideways out of habit.

Speed of running

The speed at which you run in the centre will obviously depend on your objectives and the actions of the players inside you. You must,

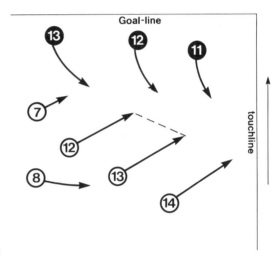

The value of straight running. The White attackers are running towards the touch-line, making it impossible for nos 7 and 8 to support but easy for the defence

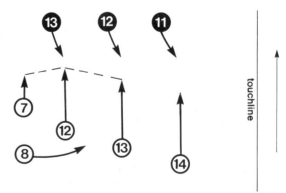

Whites are now running straight: nos 7 and 8 can get into effective support positions and create problems for the defenders

however, be aware of the need to run at a controlled pace and of the effect your running speed has on those around you. The ability to accelerate after you receive the ball is an asset and you have more options if you have something in reserve. If you are flat out, it is very difficult to side-step or to maintain all-round vision. However, this does not imply that you should run slowly; your controlled pace must still be pretty quick.

The centre in attack

As an individual attacker your basic job is to get the ball to a team-mate in a better position than yourself, ideally a try-scoring situation. At the same time, you must be ready to seize any opportunity to get past your immediate opponent. There is very little virtue in running straight into him and hoping to crash through his tackle. The outside break is the move you should cherish, as this takes you away from the cover defence and into the areas of greatest space.

The outside break is always possible if you are much faster than your opponent, but if you are not it can still be achieved if you can cause him to hesitate. Change of pace, swerve, check and go, or dummy pass inside, are all ways of causing hesitation, but for these ploys to be successful you must run fairly straight.

For an inside break to be really effective you should generally aim to move out again once you have got beyond the first tackle. To set up an inside break you have to convince your opponent that you are trying to pass him on the outside or that you are moving the ball wider. He should be aiming at your inside hip

but, if he gets across in front of you or turns his shoulders beyond you, an inside break is nearly always possible using either a side-step or a dummy pass outside. The inside break is easier if both you and the defender are on a diagonal running line.

If your attempted break fails, and you are held by an opponent, try to stay on your feet and keep the ball available for your support players. Don't make a loose or wildly optimistic pass out of contact situations. Remember, you are responsible for the ball until it is safely delivered into the hands of a team-mate. Even then your role in attack is not finished, and you must run in support whenever possible.

When you do run in support, run at the ball. That may seem obvious, but so many players

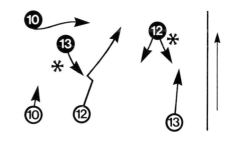

The outside break

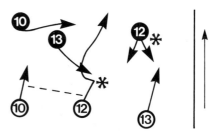

Above **The inside break**

Go for the outside break

The centre should try to stay on his feet if his break fails

run towards the ball at first but then drift away from it. If you must move away to find space, only do so when the ball is on its way to you and almost in your hands.

The centre in defence

Basically your job in defence is to tackle your immediate opponent, but it is important that you act as part of the defensive line and in accordance with your team's defensive system.

Have a positive attitude and try to force your attacker to go where you want him. Aim for his inside hip, with your tackling shoulder leading. (If you are moving right, this is your right shoulder.) Strong tackling is essential in the centre and you must never let an opponent with the ball run past your outside shoulder.

Disciplined positional play is the key to sound defence in the centre.

Discipline is important in a defensive unit

Wing threequarter

Traditionally the winger has been regarded as the chief try-scorer in a team, but also as a player who may lead a relatively lonely existence, patrolling a narrow strip of land near to the touch-line, waiting for a pass to come his way.

If this is your view of playing on the wing, then change it. The modern winger must have a complete range of skills, for there is scarcely a moment in a game when you are not likely to be involved, providing that you have a positive attitude and go looking for work.

The winger is often the main try scorer

You should have the ability to run quickly, strongly and elusively, to catch high kicks safely and to kick with both feet. Swerve, side-step and change of pace are the basic running skills you require and the high screw kick and short chip kick are your main kicking skills. You must be a sound tackler and be able to resist tackles, protect the ball and make it available to support runners when necessary. Sound positional awareness is essential in attack and defence, and you must be able to make good passes (often in an unorthodox way) when you are held by defenders. Pace is your most valuable weapon and you must constantly strive to improve your sprinting ability.

The winger in attack

In attack you are almost totally dependent on the ability and actions of the players inside you. Your most important task is to ensure that when play comes your way you are in the best position to receive a pass or run on to a kick. The ability to be in the right place at the right time is one of the hallmarks of a good winger. Don't just stand out on your side of the field waiting for things to happen – go looking for the ball on occasions. Particularly from the blind-side wing position, there are many opportunities to join in attacks, and you can often be very effective simply by running as a decoy.

When you do receive a pass you should always be prepared to try to beat your immediate opponent. Like a centre, you are usually most effective if you can run past the defender's outside shoulder, but you must not be predictable. If you receive the ball within 20 metres of your opponents' goal-line, with not more than one defender in front of you, you should always score.

Resist the temptation to kick the ball in attack unless there is plenty of space beyond the defenders and you are sure you can get to the ball before they do. A hopeful kick is usually a waste of possession. Be positive, and don't stop trying just because you are repeatedly being held or tackled. Remember, many of your team-mates will be running hard to support you, but they will soon be discouraged and stop doing so if you keep kicking or throwing the ball away carelessly when confronted by defenders.

When you are running in support outside a team-mate with the ball, maintain your depth so that when the time comes he can put the pass in front for you to run onto. Numerous scoring opportunities are lost because wingers get too flat and the final pass is either forwards or goes down to the side or even behind them. Often the passer is blamed, yet it is nearly always the winger's fault.

It is also terribly important that you have the courage to stand wide in attack so that when the ball does come your way you are running straight. The virtues of width and straight lines of running are described in the section on centre threequarter play.

The winger in defence

Tackling and dealing with attacking kicks by the opposition are your two main tasks in defence, but a third important task is providing cover defence, particularly for your full-back.

Your tackling responsibility will vary according to the type of attack you are facing and the defensive system of your team. Your basic task, however, is to ensure that your opponent does not run past you on the outside. Aim for his inside hip and try to make him run towards the touch-line. If you are not too near your own line and are confident that he is not quick enough to get away from you, it can be an advantage to delay your tackle. If you go in early he may be able to pass to a support player. If you hold off and let him almost get round you, then drive in on him towards touch – he will find it very difficult to make a pass inside.

A particular problem on the wing is that you might be faced with two attackers and no immediate support from your colleagues. Unless you are confident of knocking down body and ball, delay your tackle and force the ball-carrier to make a decision. If he decides to pass without committing you, you are then back to a one-on-one situation. If he decides to run on your inside, shadow the outside runner and hope that your cover will tackle the opponent with the ball, or turn with the ball-carrier and try to shut him off from his support runner. There are no hard-and-fast rules in such situations, but don't make it easy for the attackers. Don't commit yourself too early so that the ball-carrier doesn't have to think; and don't get caught half-way, leaving both attackers free to run past you.

You will have to deal with attacking kicks on the open side and the blind side of the field. Good positional play helped by anticipation of the attackers' intentions is the key to efficient defence. On the open side, their fly-half and inside centre are the likely kickers. Stay wide and well behind your centre, ready to cut off a

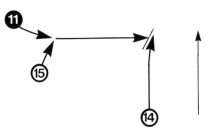

Dealing with a two-against-one attack. Try to keep both attackers outside you

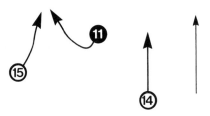

Turn in on the ball carrier and try to isolate him

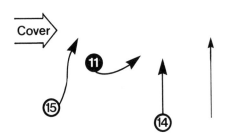

Shadow the outside player and hope the cover takes the ball carrier

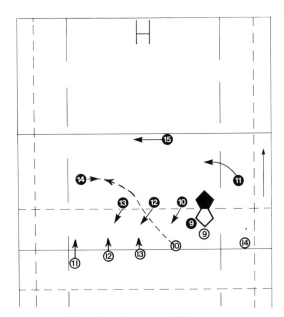

Winger dealing with a short-angled kick

long diagonal kick or to come in and gather a short, angled kick. You should only move up on your opposite winger when you are sure their inside centre is going to pass.

On the blind side, their scrum-half and fly-half are the most likely kickers. From line-outs on either side of the field, stand about 15 metres from the line-out on the 5m line until their fly-half is clearly going to pass. From scrums on your left of the field it is most likely to be their scrum-half who kicks, but on the right it will probably be the fly-half. Watching where the fly-half stands and how he takes the ball will usually give you a good indication as to how and when he is likely to kick the ball. In every match you should always quickly note which is the kicking foot favoured by opposing players.

When you do collect opposition kicks, try to turn them to your advantage whenever possible. In your own 22m area, when safety has priority, a pass to your full-back may give a better angle for the kick; but if you are under pressure, clear the ball yourself, even if it means less distance is gained. In such situations it can be an advantage if the right wing can use his left foot well and the left wing his right foot.

Outside your 22m area you should always think about counter-attack when you are presented with the ball. Don't just kick it speculatively back up the field as so many wingers seem to do. Accept the gift of possession gratefully and then try to use it constructively.

Your third main task in defence is to provide cover for your full-back. If he is waiting to catch a high ball, you should be running to a support position that will vary according to his position and where you are coming from. A good general rule, however, is to run to a position five metres directly behind the receiver. If he spills the ball you will be able to adjust and sweep it up. If he is under pressure, you should go straight in to support him, getting your hands on the ball if possible. If he has time, you can initiate a counter-attack by calling for the pass.

You must also be aware of where the main pressures from following-up attackers will come from and be prepared to carry the ball away from the danger area. Whenever your full-back goes up in attack or across in defence when the ball is moving away from you, move in towards the centre of the field ready to provide support or defence in depth if necessary.

Full-back

Full-back is probably the most exciting position in the back division.

Dealing with attacking kicks from the opposition is your main task in defence, but there are many opportunities to join in attacks from set pieces and in broken play.

A full range of skills is necessary and particularly the ability to catch kicks consistently

Full-back is an exciting position to play

and to make long, accurate kicks with either foot. Strong, fast, evasive running and the handling skills of a centre are also required, together with great courage in physically demanding situations. You must be able to tackle and resist tackles, and perform your role in rucks and mauls as well as a flanker. Above

all, you must be able to read the game to assess situations and anticipate actions so that you are always in the right place at the right time, ready to make the right decisions.

The full-back in attack

You have two main roles in attack:

1. part of a concerted back-division movement
2. an initiator of counter-attacks.

In an attacking movement by the backs, whether rehearsed or spontaneous, you should be doing any of five things:

1. joining the back line at speed to penetrate the defence
2. joining the line to provide extra support and create space for a player outside you

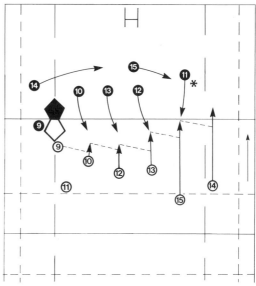

Above **The full-back in attack**

Join the back-line at speed

3. running as a decoy to draw the attention of defenders
4. running as the first support player, usually to take a pass from the winger
5. providing support in depth in case of error.

In such movements, be sure you know what you are trying to do and position yourself accordingly. All the elements of positional play described for centres and wings could apply equally to you, particularly the need for width and straight lines of running. Too many full-backs run on diagonal lines or on wide arcs. When you join the back line, try to run across the line of the ball rather than along the direction in which it is moving.

Some of your best opportunities for creative attacking play will arise from defensive situations, particularly when the opposition are kicking the ball to you or to your wings. Whenever you or your wings gather kicks, you must support each other. If you have support and space to work in, try to use the ball constructively rather than merely clear to touch or kick hopefully upfield.

The full-back in defence

Modern defensive systems rarely leave the full-back isolated as the last line of defence, but you still have a critical role to play in dealing with kicks, and in tackling. Good positional play helped by intelligent anticipation is the key to effective defence at full-back.

Whenever the opposition have the ball you must try to position yourself to cover every

eventuality. Your starting point is assessing what is likely to happen. Your judgement should be based on information you have collected before and during the game about your opponents, and on past experience in similar situations. Having quickly decided what is most likely to happen, you must position yourself accordingly, but keep some options open in case you have guessed wrongly. Inevitably your initial position will be something of a compromise, and you must constantly review and re-assess play as it develops.

Identify the main kickers on the opposing team and note which foot and type of kick they favour. Look also to see if they tend to kick

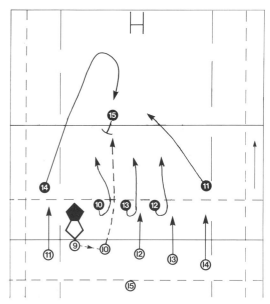

Above **Cover for the full-back from the wings dealing with a high kick**

The full-back may be the last line of defence

habitually from any particular situation. Remember always to make appropriate adjustments for weather and ground conditions. Try to out-think your opponents. If you succeed, they will make you a present of much valuable possession.

When catching and gathering kicks, you must display confidence and authority. Particularly with high balls there is often the risk of collision with other players, probably your own wingers. The general rule should be that the player going forwards to the ball is the one responsible for the catch. In such situations give a loud, early call to let everyone know that you are in the right position and accepting responsibility. Keep your eyes firmly on the ball and position your body for the next phase of action. This could mean turning your shoulders and hips towards oncoming tacklers or simply half-turning so that you can quickly kick with the appropriate foot. This aspect of positioning is all too often neglected when catching a high ball.

Given a choice, you must never let the ball bounce before gathering it. When clearing from your own 22m line, be sure to find touch when you intend to. Missing touch from this area can open the way for dangerous counter-attacks by your opponents. You must be able to screw kick

accurately and with length off either foot. Remember that on the right of the field, for example, although a left-foot kick will give you a better angle to the right touch-line, putting the ball on that foot opens you up to an on-coming tackler with the risk of a charge-down. It is sometimes necessary to sacrifice length for safety. However, it is in these situations that evasive skills like the side-step are useful in helping to create space for yourself.

The amount of tackling you have to do at full-back will largely depend upon the ability of the players in front of you and on the efficiency of your team's defensive system. When you do have to tackle it is almost always a vital tackle that must be made. The general rule is not to commit yourself to a tackle unless you have to stop an opponent running past you or you are certain you can knock down body and ball. The great art of tackling is in good positioning, getting the attacker to run where you want him to go.

If you are faced with a clean break down the centre of the field, try to force the attacker to turn inside towards the source of possession and your cover defence. If the break is wide out, push the attacker towards the touch-line, away from his support players. This may mean taking up an exaggerated position on the side, away from where you want him to go. There is always the danger that you will be beaten by sheer pace, but the more you can reduce the attacker's alternatives, the better chance you will have of stopping him. At all times, try to keep between the ball and your goal-line, though not necessarily in a straight line.

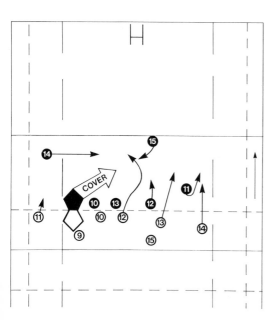

Dealing with a centre-field break

The back division in attack

Concerted attacks by the back division are essential elements in the play of every team. Such attacks must be based on the general principles of play and on the particular tactics of your team in each match. Always bearing in mind that the ultimate objective is for your team to score points, the two main functions of the back division are to initiate and develop attacks, and to support and develop attacks started by the forwards.

The ball-carrier must try to get in front of his support players

In carrying out these attacks you must try to get a ball-carrier in front of the rest of your team and ideally behind the opposition defence, and then get support to him from depth at pace. At the very least you must pose a serious threat to the defence and either cause uncertainty and hesitation in their ranks or commit individual defenders irrevocably to a course of action or line of running. Once they are committed in this way it is relatively easy to beat them by a change of running line or a pass to a colleague in space.

When initiating attacks, you must be clear about what is the target area for the main thrust and appreciate the time, space and positional needs in order for a ball-carrier to strike at that point. You must also be aware of the key decision-making moments that are likely to occur in any attack. You must recognise how different sources and types of possession increase or reduce your attacking options; your position on the field, as well as the positions of defenders and your own players, have an equally important effect.

The pace at which you carry out the attack must be appropriate for the purpose and must respond to changing circumstances, and above all the purposes and specific objectives of the attack must be clear to all your players.

Decision making

Good, early decisions must be made, and having answered the where, what, why and when

questions, the decisions about how and who must take into account the respective abilities of your players and those of the defenders. The hardest decisions to get backs to make are the personal commitments of:

1. not to kick the ball
2. to run in support.

Kicking in attack is often an admission of failure, and your priority must be to keep the ball in your hands. When you kick you immediately give away hard-earned possession, so you must try to ensure that the loss of possession is only temporary.

Continued kicking usually indicates lack of:

1. imagination
2. running speed
3. fitness.

Set moves

Attacks need a starting point, and this is where previously organised 'set moves' have a place. There has been much criticism in recent years of the utilisation of set moves and, exercised thoughtlessly, they certainly are of limited value. Use set moves merely as a starting point for your attacks, not as an end in themselves, and always consider what happens next. The main purpose of a well-rehearsed set move is to initiate an attack to try to disorganise the defence, and a move is usually employed from scrums and line-outs where the defence is also set. It is possible to call a move from secondary possession, e.g. from a ruck, but if you do, you must be sure that you have all the necessary players on their feet and in the right starting positions.

Lines of running

Alignment and, particularly, your lines of running are key factors. They should not always be the same but should vary according to the purpose and method of the attack and the source of possession.

Space

Space is your best friend, and back attacks are really all about getting a ball-carrier into space in front of your support and behind the opposition defence. At any particular moment in a match there are certain areas on the field not occupied by players. These spaces do not remain constant, but change their shape, size and position according to the movement of players. You must use your eyes and be constantly scanning the field to identify space that your team can exploit.

To get the ball across your opponents' goal-line, you need to progress through spaces. Your general approach must be to 'play into space, but not into bodies', so don't run at defenders unnecessarily and don't try to set up rucks and mauls just for the sake of it. The defenders will naturally try to fill or restrict spaces, so your basic options are to go over, through or round the defensive players.

If handling is your priority in attack, that cuts out your first option, so how do you go through or round the defence? By putting the ball into space and getting a player onto the ball? By putting a player into space and giving him the ball? By carrying the ball into space?

Before you decide on your method, your first task is to identify the potential attacking space. That space may then have to be preserved or enlarged, or a different space may need to be created. The initial space available to you will vary depending on whether the starting point for your attack is a scrum, line-out, ruck or maul, or a counter-attack from an opposition

kick. Remember, the space you are aiming for is the space behind defenders!

The back division in defence

The back division has two particular types of defensive organisation to operate: pressure defence and zone defence.

Pressure defence

In applying pressure, the basic objective is to deny the attackers space and time and to prevent the attack from reaching the gain line. It is very much a one-on-one defence, with each defender going up quickly on his opposite number to give the attacker as few options as possible. You should generally use this type of defence when your opponents are receiving slow or otherwise poor possession. Provided that there are an equal number of defenders to attackers, it is also the defensive system to use at scrums near your own line.

The fly-half and centres are the key figures in this system. They must go forwards quickly but in control, and the players nearest the source of possession should be slightly ahead of those outside. They should run for the inside hip of their opponents in such a way that the attackers have little choice but to run in the direction of the defenders' tackling shoulders.

This type of angled defensive alignment considerably reduces the potential attacking spaces between the defenders and helps to push the attack across the field. However, pressure defence is only effective if it forces the opposition to make errors, or if the defender catches attacker and ball in the tackle. There are times when it is better not to run forwards and commit yourself to tackle.

Zone defence

Zone defence is based on three principles.

1. Defenders mark areas of space rather than specific opponents.
2. The attack are allowed to have options, but in such a way that they are encouraged to

Pressure defence

make the decisions the defence wants.

3. The defenders delay and retreat until defensive reinforcements arrive and the defence can be reorganised to match the threat of the attack. Good positioning, lines of running and, above all, communication and awareness are essential to this type of defence. It is not an excuse for shirking tackles.

Try to make the attackers go where you want them to go, but don't necessarily follow your opposite number. You are responsible for a defensive corridor or channel, which extends from your inside shoulder to the inside shoulder of the next defender. Any attacker who comes into your corridor is your responsibility.

Generally speaking, you do not make a tackle unless it is necessary to stop an opponent running past your outside shoulder. The exceptions are: when you are certain that you can knock down body and ball; when two attackers perform a loop and the outside

defender steps in quickly to make the tackle; or when you know there is no cover defence on your inside.

Your main objective, however, is to maintain a defensive screen between the ball and your goal-line. If the front line of defenders do this properly the full-back is left free to sweep behind and take any extra attacker on the outside, and the blind-side winger shifts across into the mid-field to provide further cover.

This method is particularly useful at line-outs and in situations where the defenders are outnumbered by attackers. It should also be used when the team with the ball are near their own line but have time and space and are exploring the possibility of a counter-attack. If you rush forwards to tackle in such situations, it makes their decision making easy. Whatever type of defensive organisation is used, however, there comes a time when tackles have to be made. The best organisation in the world cannot hide deficiencies in tackling ability.

STRATEGY AND TACTICS

If your forwards and backs are to combine effectively in a match you must try to develop a common approach to the game and evolve a general style of play. This team strategy must be understood by all your players and be within their capabilities. It is foolish to decide upon a strategy and then expect the team to develop the skills necessary to carry it out. Your strategy should be determined according to the known strengths and weaknesses of the players in your team, as individuals and in their unit skills.

The basis of any strategy, however, will be the need to work the ball under your control into positions on the field that give your team the best chance of scoring. The team must have identified and agreed those positions and must know how they are going to score from them. This means being aware of: the players who are most likely to score; the responsibilities of each player in bringing about the scoring opportunity; and particularly the roles of the key players in any situation.

Tactics are the methods you employ to achieve your objectives in a particular match,

within the framework of the overall strategy. Tactics on the day will be influenced by the strengths and weaknesses of your opponents, by ground and weather conditions, and will take into account any disruption of your own team caused by injury or non-availability. Above all, tactics must be flexible and your team must have alternatives should the originally planned tactics not prove to be effective at the time.

Team strategy

The three basic strategic patterns of team play are those based upon forward dominance, backs' dominance with forward parity, and fifteen-man rugby.

Forward dominance

Even with a mediocre set of backs, a team can win many matches if it achieves forward dominance. Remember, getting the ball and

Forwards and backs must combine effectively during a match

keeping the ball are the first two aims of team play. If your forwards are dominant, they will certainly be able to win all their own scrum ball, most of their line-out ball and most of the ball they carry into rucks and mauls. In addition, they are likely to pick up further possession from the opposition at set-piece and broken-play situations. Keeping the ball then becomes relatively simple if you regularly use back-row moves from scrums, peels from line-outs or rolling forward drives from rucks and mauls.

You may possibly never pass the ball beyond fly-half and use your half-backs to keep the team going forwards by kicking. The rest of the backs may be used simply as support players and to maintain pressure on your opponents by sound tackling when necessary to create opportunities for your forwards to regain possession. This can be a clinically efficient strategy, but it is also usually deadly dull for at least half the team to play and for spectators to watch week after week.

Backs' dominance

It is much more difficult to be effective with a strategy based upon very good backs but relatively weak forwards. Without guaranteed good possession, the best backs in the world will find it hard to be effective throughout a game. In this situation, you have to try to use every scrap of possession effectively, which means a total commitment to running and handling, with your main point of attack always well away from the opposing forwards.

The weaknesses of this strategy are that your forwards will tend to shovel the ball back from set pieces, rucks and mauls, regardless of the situation, and it leaves you with few alternatives if things go wrong. You dare not kick because you will be giving away hard-earned possession, and you cannot hope to attack effectively close to the source of possession if you are not driving forwards in scrums, rucks and mauls. This makes it very easy for the defence to combat your attacks.

This strategy may well provide great enjoyment but will often lead to statements such as 'I'm afraid we lost – but we played all the rugby.'

Fifteen-man rugby

Ideally, therefore, every team should try to develop a balanced style of play involving all 15 players in equally important roles. Although the forwards are the primary ball winners, the backs also have a part to play through positive defence and in creating favourable conditions for the forwards to do their job. Keeping the ball and using it effectively are team responsibilities, and the team should choose its tactics carefully according to the particular situation.

Attacks must not be predictable and they should feature handling and running movements by the backs, tactical kicking at half-back, back-row attacks from scrums and driving attacks by forwards from line-outs, rucks and mauls. The point of attack must be varied and every player should be striving to go forwards, maintain continuity through good support, retain control and exert pressure on your opponents. Above all, every player must be prepared to make decisions on the field and not rely on pre-match planning and organisation.

Developing a tactical plan

The particular tactics you employ in any match must be related to your overall strategy and they must be appropriate at the time.

If you know your opponents' strengths and weaknesses beforehand, you can make some provisional pre-match decisions about how you are going to play. Once the match starts, however, you must be constantly re-appraising your opponents' and your own performance and be prepared to adjust your tactics if necessary.

Your assessment of the opposition must take into account their general pattern of play, their unit strengths and weaknesses and the individual ability of their players, particularly those in key positions. Your general policy should be to attack their weaknesses and play to your strengths. However, there are occasions when it can be useful to attack your opponents' strong points.

If, for example, they have a good back row,

Attacks must feature handling and running

your first thought may be to move the ball well away from them and make your point of attack wide out. Unfortunately, this policy often plays into their hands, as their back row will be able to get quickly away from set pieces and by strong tackling can create havoc among your back division.

If, on the other hand, you make your first attack close to the source of possession, the opposition back row will be committed to front-line defence and, provided you can maintain continuity by winning the ball from the point of contact, your back division will be relatively free from their attention when you mount your secondary attack.

Ground and weather conditions on the day should also influence your tactics. The size, slope if any, and underfoot condition of the pitch can certainly affect play, and so can sun, wind and rain. What may seem to be the obvious tactic is not necessarily the best tactic

always, so consider the implications of the prevailing conditions and all possible alternatives most carefully.

If for example, there is a strong wind behind you, there is an obvious temptation to hoist long kicks downfield, but if the opposing full-back and wings are lying deep to counter this tactic, it may prove to be a futile waste of possession. Short chips into space over the mid-field defence might be more useful kicks to try, but better still, quick passing to your wings may give them metres of clear space.

Whatever tactics you do decide upon, make sure you have some alternatives if the game does not go as you expected. It is foolish to stick to your pre-match plan if your opponents are coping easily with your efforts. On the other hand, don't abandon your tactics too readily. A team may hold you for 60 minutes but may be fully stretched to do so, and the last 20 minutes of a match often prove to be decisive.

INDEX